D1236722

NEW OXFORD ENGLISH SERIES

General Editor: A. NORMAN JEFFARES

DRYDEN

SELECTED POEMS

Chosen and edited by

JAMES KINSLEY

PROFESSOR OF ENGLISH STUDIES
UNIVERSITY OF NOTTINGHAM

OXFORD UNIVERSITY PRESS

1963

Oxford University Press, Amen House, London E.C. 4

GLASGOW NEW YORK TORONTO MELBOURNE WELLINGTON
BOMBAY CALCUTTA MADRAS KARACHI LAHORE DACCA
CAPE TOWN SALISBURY NAIROBI IBADAN ACCRA
KUALA LUMPUR HONG KONG

Cover portrait by Leonard Rosoman

PRINTED IN GREAT BRITAIN
AT THE UNIVERSITY PRESS, OXFORD
BY VIVIAN RIDLER
PRINTER TO THE UNIVERSITY

CONTENTS

INTRODUCTION

DRYDEN left Cambridge after graduation in 1654 and, on a moderate income from landed property left to him by his father, settled in London. While at college, says a contemporary, he

was reckoned a man of good parts and learning [and had] read over and very well understood all the Greek and Latin poets . . . but his head was too roving and active . . . to confine himself to a college life; so he . . . went to London into gayer company, and set up for a poet.[1]

But the times were not propitious for poetry. Dryden probably worked for a time as secretary to his cousin Sir Gilbert Pickering, then in Cromwell's service; and after Cromwell's death he is said to have 'Writ Prefaces for Meat and Drink' in the pay of Herringman, who was to be his own publisher from 1660 until 1678. He had begun to write verse while still at Westminster School; but his first significant poem is the *Heroique Stanza's* on the death of Cromwell, in which already he shows his characteristic assurance and his skill in panegyric.

In 1660, with the more judicious of those who had been in the service of Cromwell, he shifted his political allegiance; and began to make a literary reputation with a series of poems celebrating the Restoration. He moved into royalist circles through a friendship with Sir Robert Howard, son of the Earl of Berkshire, and later in his marriage with Howard's sister Elizabeth. *Annus Mirabilis* (1667) was written at the Howard family house in Wiltshire. This fine modern georgic on the Great Fire and the naval war of 1666, heralding the prosperity of England under a benign Providence and the new king,

[1] See Dryden, *Poems*, ed. W. D. Christie and C. H. Firth, 1893, p. xvi.

established Dryden as a national poet. In 1668 he became poet laureate and historiographer royal.

He discovered early, however, that the rewards of court service were uncertain; and he began to write for the reopened theatres, which promised more security to a professional man of letters. After two attempts in comedy—*The Wild Gallant* (1663) and *The Rival Ladies* (1664)—he turned with Robert Howard to a novel form of high verse drama in *The Indian Queen. A Tragedy*, and made his first independent contribution to the heroic play with a sequel, *The Indian Emperour* (1665). This and two later plays—*Tyrannick Love* (1669) and *The Conquest of Granada* (1671)—fed the public appetite for stage rhetoric and lavish spectacle, and gave Dryden a central place in the world of the theatre. He established himself too in the comedy of sexual intrigue with a series of plays based on French models—*Secret Love* (1667), *Sir Martin Mar-All* (1667), and *An Evening's Love* (1668); but after the triumph of *Marriage A-la-Mode* in 1672 his talent for witty dramatic repartee declined into tedious indecency. 'I confess,' he wrote as early as 1668,

my chief endeavours are to delight the age in which I live. If the humour of this be for low comedy, small accidents, and raillery, I will force my genius to obey it. . . . I know I am not so fitted by nature to write comedy: I want that gaiety of humour which is required to it. My conversation is slow and dull; my humour saturnine, and reserved. . . . So that those who decry my comedies do me no injury, except it be in point of profit.[1]

He felt a growing sense of inadequacy even, despite his commercial success, in the heroic play. In the Dedication of *Aureng-Zebe* (1675), his last attempt in this genre, he says:

I desire to be no longer the *Sisyphus* of the Stage; to rowl up a Stone

---

[1] *Defence of An Essay of Dramatick Poesy*, 1668.

with endless labour. . . which is perpetually falling down again; I never thought my self very fit for an Employment, where many of my Predecessors have excell'd me in all kinds.

It was in the theatre, with the anti-Dutch tragedy *Amboyna* (1673), that Dryden first tried his hand at political satire; and the growing interest in opera tempted him, with deplorable results, to turn *Paradise Lost* to libretto in *The State of Innocence* (1677; probably for a court performance only). But his greatest achievement in the 1670's was with a form of drama that brought together the native tradition in poetry and characterization with the French neo-classical principle of 'the Unities of Time, Place, and Action . . . more exactly . . . than perhaps the English theatre requires'. In *All for Love* (1677) he recast Shakespeare's *Antony and Cleopatra*, extending the final phase of the play into a five-act tragedy of love in the convention of the Restoration stage. The new structure limited his range of action and feeling, and reduced the complexity —and indeed the human appeal—of the central characters. Here, and in Dryden's adaptation of *Troilus and Cressida* (1679), the dehydration of Shakespeare's poetry to satisfy modern taste is as great a loss as the simplification of character; but *All for Love* is the finest tragedy of its time, and the most successful English experiment in high drama on the French model.[1]

Dryden's work for the theatre had three important by-products: a series of lyrics, many of which remained popular (in themselves and as song models) far into the eighteenth century; a long sequence of critical essays; and a superb collection of prologues and epilogues. Most of the essays are prefaces and dedications published with the plays (criticism had not yet become a kind of writing either self-sufficient or profitable). They deal, partly in imitation of Corneille's

[1] Cf. M. E. Prior, *The Language of Tragedy*, 1947.

prefaces, with problems that confronted Dryden as a working dramatist: the heroic play, blank verse and rhyme, the
dramatic kinds, the unities, morality, and stage diction. The
most ambitious essay, and Dryden's only piece of formal
criticism, is the Ciceronian dialogue *Of Dramatick Poesie*
(1668). This is a defence of English drama against the ad-
vocates of the classical and neo-classical traditions, built round
the definition of a play as 'a just and lively Image of Human
Nature, representing its Passions and Humours, and the
Changes of Fortune to which it is subject, for the Delight and
Instruction of Mankind'; and it contains an 'examen' of Ben
Jonson's *Silent Woman*—the first piece of analysis in English.
Dryden's essays, indeed, mark the beginning of modern
English criticism:[1] nothing in their style, as Johnson says,

is cold or languid; the whole is airy, animated, and vigorous: what is
little is gay; what is great is splendid. . . . Every thing is excused by
the play of images and the spriteliness of expression. Though all is
easy, nothing is feeble; though all seems careless, there is nothing
harsh; and though since his earlier works more than a century has
passed they have nothing yet uncouth or obsolete.[2]

In the prologues and epilogues Dryden's talent for verse talk
is fully exercised in comic monologue, social and political
comment, graceful eulogy, and critical discourse. We are
apt nowadays to undervalue these occasional verses: but to
speak a prologue, says Colley Cibber, was considered 'one of
the hardest Parts, and strongest Proofs of sound Elocution';
and a glance at the records of the Restoration theatre shows
that this was a privilege coveted by the best actors.[3] The
principle of decorum applied here, as in all Dryden's work.

[1] The most recent general discussion is George Watson's, in *Of Dramatic
Poesy and other Critical Essays*, 2 vols., 1962.

[2] *Lives of the English Poets*, ed. G. B. Hill, 1905, i. 418.

[3] On the history and vogue of the prologue, see A. N. Wiley, *Rare Prologues
and Epilogues (1642–1700)*, 1940.

He served a great range of occasions and audiences with constant poetic propriety. Whether he is celebrating a public event, flattering distinguished listeners, explaining a critical principle illustrated in the play, or winning an audience to his side in broad comedy, his approach to prologue and epilogue is serious and dramatic. He appreciates the humours, preferences, and weaknesses of theatre audiences with a thoroughness unequalled in the history of our drama; he understands the value of the prologue convention to a professional playwright who must please to live; and he exploits audience and literary form with complete assurance.

By 1680 Dryden, tired and dissatisfied by writing for the stage, unhappy in his relations with the theatre, and outpaced by a new generation of dramatists, was turning more and more to poetry. His later plays—some written in the royal service, but most to relieve the poverty of his age after the fall of the Stewarts in 1688—have little intrinsic merit, though he has a place beside Purcell in the history of English opera. In the year when his dramatic writing reached its climax in *All for Love*, he began to display his power in mock-heroic satire with *Mac Flecknoe* (see p. 58).

His main chance came in 1681 when, it is said, the king asked him to celebrate the defeat of the Whigs in a satiric poem. The application of David and Absalom to current English politics was no novelty: Dryden's achievement in *Absalom and Achitophel* (see pp. 44, 66), in an age with a taste for *histoires travesties*, was the imaginative heroic-satiric elaboration of these parallels on the grand scale. There is little action in the poem; it has been suggestively compared to a masterpiece of 'history painting', its canvas 'crowded with figures, clearly divided into two opposing groups and painted in varying perspective'.[1] It opens with a narrative, sketches of the

[1] Ian Jack, *Augustan Satire 1650–1750*, 1952, p. 73. For a fuller discussion of

protagonists, and the dialogue in which Achitophel seduces
Absalom; a series of satiric portraits of Whig personalities is
followed by Dryden's own exposition of the main political
issue; and that is supplemented by a contrasting series of portraits of the king's friends. The main purpose of *Absalom and
Achitophel* is the vindication of Charles II: the heroic style—in
which, says Dryden, 'the Plot, the Characters, the Wit, the
Passions, the Descriptions, are all exalted above the level of
common converse, as high as the imagination of the Poet can
carry them'[1]—is appropriate, both to biblical allegory and to
a narrative of momentous public events.[2] The characterization
is as elevated as the style; not only in the celebration of political virtue in the king's friends, but in portraying Absalom like
a character from heroic drama, torn between honour and
ambition, duty and passion, and even in the representation of
Achitophel with the diabolical energy and ability of Milton's
Satan. Both Absalom and Achitophel exemplify—one seriously, the other satirically—the tragic character as Dryden
had described it:

> As for a perfect character of virtue, it never was in Nature. . . .
> There are alloys of frailty to be allowed for the chief persons, yet so
> that the good which is in them shall outweigh the bad, and con-
> sequently leave room for punishment on the one side and pity on the
> other.[3]

Absalom and Achitophel is much more than a satire in the
restricted modern sense, though Dryden later called it such
and thought the satiric 'character' of Zimri (see pp. 46–47),
moving beautifully between ambivalent pity and casual

the points made in this paragraph see the introduction and notes to *Absalom
and Achitophel*, ed. James and Helen Kinsley, 1961.

[1] *Of Dramatick Poesie*, 1668.

[2] Cf. Preface to *Annus Mirabilis*, an 'historical' poem in which 'both the
Actions and the Actors are as much Heroick, as any Poem can contain'.

[3] Preface to *Troilus and Cressida*, 1679.

contempt, 'worth the whole Poem'. It is a heroic amalgam, after the manner in which Dryden supposed the Roman satirist Varro to have written, of 'a kind of mirth, and gayety' blended with 'many things . . . drawn from the very intrails of Philosophy, and many things . . . severely argu'd'—history, propaganda and satire, panegyric, and political discourse.

If it be considered [says Dr. Johnson] as a poem political and controversial it will be found to comprise all the excellences of which the subject is susceptible: acrimony of censure, elegance of praise, artful delineation of characters, variety and vigour of sentiment, happy turns of language, and pleasing harmony of numbers; and all these raised to such a height as can scarcely be found in any other English composition.[1]

Satire itself, Dryden came to believe—partly, I think, in the evolution of the complex novelty of *Absalom and Achitophel* —is a species of heroic poetry gaining its subtlest effects not by abuse but by irony:

The nicest and most delicate touches of Satire consist in fine Raillery. This . . . must be inborn, it must proceed from a Genius, and particular way of thinking, which is not to be taught. . . . How easie it is to call Rogue and Villain, and that wittily! But how hard to make a Man appear a Fool, a Blockhead, or a Knave, without using any of those opprobrious terms! . . . This is the Mystery of that Noble Trade. . . . There is still a vast difference betwixt the slovenly Butchering of a Man, and the fineness of a stroak that separates the Head from the Body, and leaves it standing in its place.[2]

Dryden pours new wine into many old bottles, extending the range and improving the quality of accepted forms. The formal satire which the Elizabethans, in imitative zeal, introduced from Latin literature, had become established as a poetic kind; and the time was propitious for perfecting it in English. Political and religious controversy were fertile

[1] Op. cit. i. 436.   [2] *Discourse concerning Satire*, 1693.

themes; professional writers turned their attention profitably to personalities and manners; the art of couplet verse, the inevitable medium for satire, had been brought to a high technical finish in panegyrical and occasional poetry; and the art of satiric 'character' or type-portraiture had been refined in both prose and verse.[1] Dryden was not an innovator in the writing of formal satire; but he raised the tradition established by the Elizabethans, and developed by Butler, Marvell, and Oldham, to a new level of art, and enabled his Augustan successors to make it a central poetic mode.

Dryden's emphasis on the artistic delightfulness of satire was timely, and is of the first importance to the study of his craft. Traditionally, the satirist claims a moral justification for his work; but the effect of good satire—'the fine art of calling names'—is pleasurable, not corrective. The vein of malice in human nature is not in itself satiric, but it underlies satire; and when artistic devices are used to intensify and refine that malice, the purely artistic motive tends to supervene. A satirist of men and manners, to confirm his right to criticize, must give his criticism the sanction of moral concern. But that concern is not necessarily dominant or even sincere. The true moralist is corrective and constructive; the literary satirist, on the other hand, has a primary loyalty to his art. It has never mattered much to him 'to what lies he has stooped, so long as he moralised his song'.[2] He must feel concerned for what he writes; he need not feel strongly on what he writes about; and it is to this artistic sincerity that Dryden points. As long as satire was justified only in its moral effects, and as long as the satiric couplet was employed only by men of ill temper, private grudge, or sober corrective purpose, satire could never become a main literary kind.

[1] See D. Nichol Smith, *Characters of the Seventeenth Century*, 1918.
[2] A. M. Clark, *Studies in Literary Modes*, 1946, p. 42.

Dryden had a genius for deploying a varied artillery and for directing a combined fire that destroys evenly and utterly all along the line. His satiric method is never simple; he uses the whole range of colours in the satiric spectrum. Panegyric, mock-heroic characterization, argument, irony, sarcasm, naked abuse—all these are turned to advantage. He had at his command in the couplet an instrument of great flexibility, with which he was powerfully at ease; he had a gift for rhetoric, a strong, masculine utterance, and a volatile sense of fun. These advantages, together with his conception of satire as a high poetic kind, helped him to find fuller expression in this than in any other poetic mode.

The seventeenth-century association of political and religious allegiances, and the religious motivation in the exclusionist crisis of 1679–81, made it natural that Dryden should take a public part in theological controversy. In *Religio Laici* (1682) he discusses the problem of authority in religion in a simple 'legislative' style: a man, he says, 'is to be cheated into Passion, but to be reason'd into Truth' without seductive rhetoric.

This . . . is a composition of great excellence in its kind, in which the familiar is very properly diversified with the solemn, and the grave with the humorous; in which metre has neither weakened the force nor clouded the perspicuity of argument: nor will it be easy to find another example equally happy of this middle kind of writing, which, though prosaick in some parts, rises to high poetry in others.[1]

The poem is of much ideological interest. Dryden stands in the sceptical or 'Pyrrhonist' tradition, setting limits to human reason as a guide to ultimate truth, but criticizing both the Roman claim to infallibility and the Protestant dependence on Scripture interpreted by individual judgement.[2] The position

[1] Johnson, op. cit. i. 442.
[2] For a full discussion see Louis I. Bredvold, *The Intellectual Milieu of John Dryden*, 1934.

he takes up is a compromise: he accepts what doctrine the Scriptures and the Fathers have established, and urges (in religion as in politics) the restraint of 'private Reason' in the interests of 'Common Quiet'.

But the compromise was, and could be, only temporary. It has commonly been supposed that Dryden's conversion to the Roman Church in 1686–7 was a piece of political 'trimming': that when the crown passed to a Papist the poet laureate prudently moved with it. Yet his movement from *Religio Laici* to *The Hind and the Panther* (1687) was a quite logical process, from uneasy anti-rationalism to the complete acceptance of Catholic authority.[1] *The Hind and the Panther*, rather casually designed in the tradition of the medieval beast fable, is not formally a success. The animal disputants, representing the Roman and Anglican churches, seem unnecessary to the development of the apologetic. But it offers a great variety of style and matter—historical narrative, satire on the Reformation and the sects that were spawned from it, an elaborate and self-sufficient allegory (also in beast-fable form) of current church politics, satiric 'characters', and some of the finest verse argument in the language.

Dryden recognized that 'English poetry, if it were to develop, must recover some of the properties of prose . . . which . . . it was in danger of losing, those especially of clarity, directness of statement, immediacy of effect and of nervous

---

[1] Cf. Scott, *Works of Dryden*, 1808, i. 308: He 'seems to have doubted with such a strong wish to believe, as, accompanied with circumstances of extrinsic influence, led him finally into the opposite extreme of credulity. His view of the doctrines of Christianity, and of its evidence, were such as could not legitimately found him in the conclusions he draws [in *Religio Laici*] in favour of the Church of England; and accordingly, in adopting them, he evidently stretches his complaisance towards the national religion, while perhaps in his heart he was even then disposed to think there was no middle course between natural religion and the church of Rome.'

strength and suppleness'.[1] Of this, *Religio Laici* and *The Hind and the Panther* are good illustrations. But there is, besides, a deal of *poetic* logic in them. Dryden's arguments lack coherence and depth: he has not the breadth of mind, or the eye for significant detail in argument, that the apologist needs. But the illumination of argument by rhetoric, by exaltation of tone and by satiric thrusts, has here a varied poetic pattern with an appeal and conviction of its own. Mark Van Doren hints at the proper approach when he says that these poems cannot be considered in fragments: their strength lies 'in what De Quincey called their "sequaciousness". They must be known in all their ins and outs before they can begin to impress.'[2] Their essential unity is not formal but stylistic. The darkness and light, the flats and elevations, the subtle shifts in tone from the familiar or satiric to the majestic, are the real sources of Dryden's persuasive power.

He wrote a considerable amount of prose, political and historical, in the 1680's; and some of his finest verse panegyric belongs also to this decade of his maturity. To appreciate this strand in his work demands historical imagination and sympathy. He had, says Dr Johnson,

all forms of excellence, intellectual and moral, combined in his mind, with endless variation. . . . He considers the great as entitled to encomiastick homage, and brings praise rather as a tribute than a gift, more delighted by the fertility of his invention than mortified by the prostitution of his judgment.[3]

His official praise, says Mark Van Doren,

rings with a round Roman grandeur. He writes as if he lived to praise, not praised to live. His lines speak contempt for all things small—small passions, small deeds, small wit. . . . And his resources are infinite.[4]

[1] Bonamy Dobrée, *Variety of Ways*, 1932, p. 9.
[2] *The Poetry of John Dryden*, 1931, p. 179.
[3] Op. cit. i. 399–400.   [4] Op. cit., p. 117.

These comments touch on a fundamental aspect of Dryden's panegyrics, and indeed of the attitudes of his time. His realism and his observation of men, in his comedies and satires, exemplify the lucid matter-of-factness—in many reduced to a brutal insensitiveness to principle—which is typical of the age. But Restoration England was resolved to be, if not the nursery, the forcing-house of the heroic virtues. The 'spotted actuality' of human nature could be counteracted and transcended by a constant representation of the ideal. Dryden's recognition of the false chivalry, the empty heroics, and the pretence to principle in political and court life, is reflected in the sustained mock-heroic of *Absalom and Achitophel*; but there is on the other hand little suggestion of mere pretence, little essential artificiality, in the best of his poetic drama. The real and the poetic do not always correspond. Poetry can do better than nature—a venerable thesis, the Renaissance development of the Aristotelian notion that art is perfect and universal, which Dryden himself restates in the *Parallel of Poetry and Painting*. The artist should 'form to himself an idea of perfect nature':

thereby correcting Nature from what actually she is in individuals, to what she ought to be, and what she was created. . . . An ingenious flattery is to be allowed to the professors of both arts, so long as the likeness is not destroyed. . . .

Though it must be an idea of perfection, from which both the epic poet and the history painter draws, yet all perfections are not suitable to all subjects; but every one must be designed according to that perfect beauty which is proper to him.[1]

In poetry lies the antidote to the weaknesses and imperfections of the world. Adulation becomes a justifiable art; and in its art lies its justification. Dryden elevated his imperfect human subjects to the level of ideal exemplars. His panegyrics are less

[1] *Essays*, ed. W. P. Ker, 1900, ii. 125, 127.

hymns on individual men and women than celebrations of the virtues they typify. The 'spotted actuality' is lost in the ideal which the poet creates; and in this creation, extravagance and hyperbolical compliment play a main part. Dryden's exaggerations have a strict poetic function; they are part of the 'propriety' of panegyric. He is continuing a Renaissance tradition: Ben Jonson, in his conversations with Drummond, observed that

> Donnes Anniversarie was profane and full of Blasphemies . . . he told Mr Donne, if it had been written of the Virgin Marie it had been something; to which he answered that he described the Idea of a Woman, and not as she was.[1]

That Dryden flattered for his own ends is obvious enough, but flattery and the display of wit were not his only motives. His satiric portraits belong to a freer, broader, and more colourful world than the reality of Restoration politics; and what is true of these is no less true of his idealized eulogies. Art distorts and heightens for praise and blame alike.

In 1680, with a collaborative translation of Ovid's *Epistles*, Dryden began the work which was to absorb the energies of his last years. He contributed to the early volumes of Tonson's poetical miscellany (1684, 1685, 1693) some of his best criticism—both on the art of translation and on the major classical poets—and a mass of translation from Ovid, Theocritus, Lucretius, Homer, Horace, and Virgil. In 1693 he edited a version of the *Satires* of Juvenal and Persius, contributing all of Persius and five Juvenalian satires himself, with a long discourse on the history and art of satire. Four years later he

---

[1] *Ben Jonson*, ed. C. H. Herford and Percy Simpson, i (1925), p. 133. Cf. Dryden on his portrait of John Driden of Chesterton: 'I think I have not onely drawn the features of my worthy Kinsman, but have also given my Own Opinion, of what an Englishman in Parliament ought to be; & deliver it as a Memorial of my own Principles to all Posterity' (*Letters*, ed. C. E. Ward, 1942, p. 120).

completed his translation of *The Works of Virgil*, again with
a major critical essay; and in 1700, just before his death, he
published *Fables Ancient and Modern . . . from Homer, Ovid,
Boccace, and Chaucer*, with the most personal and delightful of
all his prefaces.

Dryden defended, and practised, the art of 'paraphrase, or
translation with latitude': in 'litteral, and close Translation . . .
the Poet is confin'd so streightly to his Author's Words, that
he wants elbow-room, to express his Elegancies'.[1] His chief
concern was to preserve the character of his original. He felt
free in this to omit phrases and images that 'wou'd not appear
so shining in the *English*'; and where he enlarged on an ancient
author, he says,

> I desire the false Criticks wou'd not always think that those
> thoughts are wholly mine, but that either they are secretly in the Poet,
> or may be fairly deduc'd from him: or at least, if both these consi-
> derations should fail, that my own is of a piece with his, and that if
> he were living, and an *Englishman*, they are such, as he wou'd prob-
> ably have written.[2]

From Tudor times translators had been transforming classical poets into Englishmen, but Dryden's policy is freshly
critical and systematic.[3]

> The affluence and comprehension of our language [says Johnson]
> is very illustriously displayed in our poetical translations of ancient
> writers: a work . . . which we were long unable to perform with
> dexterity. . . . Cowley saw that . . . 'copyers' were a 'servile race';
> he asserted his liberty, and spread his wings so boldly that he left his
> authors. It was reserved for Dryden to fix the limits of poetical
> liberty, and give us just rules and examples of translation.[4]

His aim was to make his original 'appear as charming as he

---

[1] Dedication of *Examen Poeticum*, 1693.   [2] Preface to *Sylvae*, 1685.
[3] Parts of this and later paragraphs are reprinted, with some change, from
my introduction to *The Works of Virgil*, 1961.   [4] Op. cit. i. 421–2.

possibly can', speaking 'that kind of *English*, which he would have spoken, had he lived in *England*, and had written to this Age'. Dryden and his Augustan successors understood that translation is, at its most refined, an art of analogy: of 'reviving the old of past ages to the present' by shaping it again in a modern linguistic and cultural mould. So Pope took Trumbull's advice, in a letter of 9 April 1708, to make Homer 'speak good *English*, to dress his admirable characters in . . . proper, significant, and expressive conceptions, and to make his works as useful and instructive to this degenerate age, as he was to our friend *Horace*, when he read him at Praeneste'. When such an ideal is realized, the gap between original and translation becomes insignificant. The ancient poet is again culturally effective, and the translator is his 'noble collateral'.

Dryden experimented with the translation of Ovid for twenty years, attempting 'to restore . . . his Native sweetness, easiness, and smoothness; and to give my Poetry a kind of Cadence . . . as like the Original, as the *English* can come up to the *Latin*'.[1] He was attracted by Ovid's facility in portraying 'the movements and affections of the mind', his urbanity—he wrote, 'as the *French* call it, *cavalièrement*'—and by his wit; and Dryden spoke of his Ovidian translations as 'the best of all my endeavours in this kind. . . . Perhaps . . . he was more according to my Genius.' Although he cannot adequately represent the impassioned rhetoric of Ovid, and too freely elaborates the Ovidian conceit with inept ingenuity, Dryden succeeds in pastoral passages, and in accounts of battle. In the song of Polyphemus, for instance, Ovid weaves a delicate harmony in repeated sounds on a framework of metrical iteration:

> Candidior nivei folio, Galatea, ligustri;
> floridior pratis; longa procerior alno;

[1] Dedication of *Examen Poeticum*, 1693.

> splendidior vitro; tenero lascivior haedo;
> laevior assiduo detritis aequore conchis;
> solibus hibernis, aestiva gratior umbra;
> nobilior pomis . . .

Dryden (see p. 131, 'Oh lovely *Galatea*', &c.), in his smooth rhythms, and indeed through the resistance of the couplet to the pointed concentration of the Latin, produces a level grace and a sustained lyricism as fine as the original. In describing fights—which he does with the enthusiastic violence common in poets who have not seen military service—Dryden perhaps discovers more jocularity and playful fancy in Ovid than he ought. But despite occasional lapses into burlesque, his *bravura* makes the English *Metamorphoses* exhilarating reading (see pp. 125–7).

He penetrated the double secret of Horace's style in the odes —the *curiosa felicitas* and simple grace of his diction, and the brisk vigour, 'jollity, and . . . good humour' of his literary character. Much of Horace's delicacy, especially in the disposition and choice of epithets, is lost in translation—what was within the reach of Ben Jonson, Herrick, or Marvell was too subtle for Dryden—but he found Horace's philosophy congenial, and manages his informal, colloquial manner admirably (see pp. 104–5).

Two elements in the style of Lucretius appealed to Dryden: 'a certain kind of noble pride, and positive assertion . . . with so much scorn and indignation' in philosophical argument, and 'the perpetual torrent of his verse'.[1] He responded naturally to Lucretius; and although the Lucretian thunder was too heavy and sustained for him[2]—it could be echoed in English

---

[1] Preface to *Sylvae*, 1685.
[2] Cf. Lucretius, iii. 833–7, and Dryden:

> ad confligendum venientibus undique Poenis,
> omnia cum belli trepido concussa tumultu

only by a Miltonic weight and complexity—the simple
exposition and majestic declamation of the Latin, especially
when a thread of satire runs through it, were exactly suited
to Dryden's own manner.

Dryden's critique of Juvenal is the eulogy of an enthusiast:
compared with Horace,

> *Juvenal* is of a more vigorous and Masculine Wit, he gives me as
> much Pleasure as I can bear: He fully satisfies my Expectation, he
> Treats his Subject home: His Spleen is rais'd, and he raises mine:
> I have the Pleasure of Concernment in all he says; He drives his
> Reader along with him.[1]

Dryden responded to the heroic quality in Juvenal's satire—
the epic parody and imitation, the investment of invective
with the qualities that Cicero prescribes for the grand style,
'vehemens, acer, ardens, gravis, grandiloquus, asper, tristis'.
He cannot represent, in the couplet, the weight and emphasis
of the Latin line: 'quicquid agunt homines, votum, timor, ira,
voluptas, gaudia, discursus . . .' is weakly rendered in 'What
Humane Kind desires, and what they shun, / Rage, Passions,
Pleasures, Impotence of Will . . .'. Dryden misses much of
Juvenal's sentiment, and the touches of colour and depth in
his poetry. Yet the couplet form brings a new, different kind
of force to Juvenal, satirically more effective than the heavy

> horrida contremuere sub altis aetheris oris,
> in dubioque fuere utrorum ad regna cadendum
> omnibus humanis esset terraque marique. . . .

> When Punique arms infested Land and Main,
> When Heav'n and Earth were in confusion hurl'd,
>   For the debated Empire of the World,
> Which aw'd with dreadful expectation lay,
>   Sure to be Slaves, uncertain who shou'd sway. . . .

[1] *Discourse concerning Satire*, 1693.

hexameter, in patterns of alliteration, repetition, and anti-
thesis:

> sunt quas eunuchi inbelles ac mollia semper
> oscula delectent et desperatio barbae. . . .

> There are, who in soft Eunuchs, place their Bliss;
> To shun the scrubbing of a Bearded Kiss. . . .

> visne salutari sicut Seianus, habere
> tantundem, atque illi summas donare curules,
> illum exercitibus praeponere . . .?

> Now tell me truly, wou'dst thou change thy Fate
> To be, like him, first Minister of State?
> To have thy Levees Crowded with resort,
> Of a depending, gaping, servile Court:
> Dispose all Honours, of the Sword and Gown,
> Grace with a Nod, and Ruin with a Frown . . .?[1]

Dryden found Persius much more troublesome to translate.
His 'grande sophos' called for the same elevation as Juvenal's
sublimity did, but his obscure diction and 'scabrous and hob-
bling Verse' were awkward for the translator. If Dryden does
manage to make Persius speak as 'if he were living, and an
Englishman', it is through epigrammatic skill and a faculty for
hard, bold, colloquial statement.

With the example of Virgil before him, and many Renais-
sance precedents, Dryden had an early ambition to write (like
Milton) a heroic poem 'chiefly for the Honour of my Native
Country'. But

being encourag'd only with fair Words, by King *Charles* II, my little
Sallary ill paid, and no prospect of a future Subsistence, I was then
Discourag'd in the beginning of my Attempt; and now Age has over-
taken me; and Want, a more insufferable Evil, through the Change of
the Times [the Revolution of 1688], has wholly disenabl'd me.[2]

---

[1] Juvenal, *Sat.* vi. 366–8, x. 90–92; Dryden, vi. 483–5, x. 144–9.
[2] *Discourse concerning Satire*, 1693.

The translation of the *Aeneid* was as near as he came to realizing his ambition. He had no mean idea of his task. The Postscript to the Reader has a noble and earnest simplicity, an awareness of inadequacy tempering his sense of achievement, that recalls Milton's declaration of his poetic ideals and looks forward to Johnson's Preface to his *Dictionary*:

> What *Virgil* wrote in the vigour of his Age, in Plenty and at Ease, I have undertaken to Translate in my Declining Years: strugling with Wants, oppress'd with Sickness, curb'd in my Genius, lyable to be misconstrued in all I write. . . . Yet steady to my Principles, and not dispirited with my Afflictions, I have, by the Blessing of God on my Endeavours, overcome all difficulties. . . . For, what I have done, Imperfect as it is, will be judg'd in after Ages, and possibly in the present, to be no dishonour to my Native Country; whose Language and Poetry wou'd be more esteem'd abroad, if they were better understood.

Dryden's knowledge of the Latin poets and their language was, for his time, both extensive and exact; and his critical comments on Virgil, as on his other 'originals', are admirably perceptive. But when confronted with Virgil's poetry, he despaired. Close translation, he says, is made impossible by the qualitative differences between Latin, 'a most severe and compendious language', and English; and Virgil's Latin in particular has a richness and concentration beyond the scope of any modern language. Of brevity and elegance, the two essential Virgilian qualities, the first defies translation; and Dryden was forced to concentrate on preserving the second as best he could. Virgil's Latin is like ambergris, 'a Rich Perfume, but of so close and glutinous a Body, that it must be open'd with inferiour scents of Musk or Civet, or the sweetness will not be drawn out'. His diction called on Dryden 'in every line for some new word: and I paid so long, that I was almost Banckrupt'.

Virgil's art of subtle compression, of evoking a rich com-
plication of primary meaning and suggestion in word-patterns,
sets him apart from Dryden; and in syntax the texture of
Dryden's verse is looser than Virgil's. There is, moreover, a
fundamental difference in the poetic personalities of the two
poets. In temper as in style Dryden stands closer to Homer, as
he himself recognized. Virgil, he says,

was of a quiet, sedate Temper; *Homer* was violent, impetuous, and
full of Fire. The chief Talent of *Virgil* was Propriety of Thoughts, and
Ornament of Words; Homer was rapid in his thoughts, and took all
the Liberties . . . allow'd him: *Homer*'s Invention was more copious,
Virgil's more confin'd. . . . One warms you by Degrees; the other sets
you on fire all at once, and never intermits his Heat. . . . This Vehe-
mence of [*Homer*'s], I confess, is more suitable to my Temper.[1]

A Homeric ardour, sophisticated and controlled by Augustan
rhetoric, is the essence of Dryden's style. He is a poet of
muscle and sinew, delighting in action, in violent feeling, and
in strong and final utterance. In his *Æneis* he shows some
uneasiness and impatience with Virgil's grave artistry, and
makes spasmodic attempts to give the poem his own natural
pith and heat. The Latin, says Scott, restrained him 'to a
correct, steady, and even flight, . . . damped his energy by its
regularity, and fettered his excursive imagination by the
sobriety of its decorum'. But Dryden's paraphrastic method
gave him licence enough; he is ever adding detail to increase
the vitality of the narrative, especially in scenes of slaughter,
where he often comes nearer to Ovid than to Virgil.

Much of the vulgarity and colloquialism in the *Æneis* is
deliberate, for Dryden had a fine sense of propriety in diction.
I suspect he found stretches of Virgil a bore, and the maintenance of the Latin 'majesty in the midst of plainness' a strain.
He had admitted long before, in a discussion of tragi-comedy,

[1] Preface to *Fables*, 1700.

that 'continued gravity keeps the spirit too much bent; we must refresh it sometimes, as we bait on a journey, that we may go on with greater ease'. The alloy of common speech and indecorous wit does not detract from the strength of his heroic style, and it is a carping purist who protests much.

Professor C. S. Lewis condemns the humanist misconception of Latin poetry that Dryden inherited, 'the spectral solemnity, the gradus epithets, the dictionary language'.[1] But a diction removed from the colloquial and consecrated by poetic tradition was one of Virgil's own aims; and in Dryden's *Virgil*, as in Pope's *Homer*, a measure of artifice in language gives 'a certain ritual ceremony and a certain temporal distance to events and manners and modes of belief which could not be contemporary'.[2] Yet Dryden was not seriously infected with spectral solemnity and dictionary language. In his colloquialisms, in occasional satiric intrusions, and in moments of sheer burlesque, he runs deliberately counter to the neoclassical tradition of the epic.[3] Dr. Tillyard has suggested that the 'addition of the burlesque to the serious', as early as *Annus Mirabilis*, 'is potentially Dryden's original contribution to the course of the English epic', implying for him and for his age 'a high degree of self-consciousness, the refusal to be ultimately committed'.[4] This ambivalent attitude to the heroic is displayed in Dryden's verse satires, in his translations of Homer, Boccaccio, and Chaucer, and even in the *Æneis*.

The *Virgil* is of great historical importance. Dryden, perhaps even more than Milton, set the tone in style and diction for the elevated kinds of Augustan poetry; and this book has left its mark on eighteenth-century heroic, mock-heroic,

[1] *English Literature in the Sixteenth Century*, 1954, p. 84.

[2] Bonamy Dobrée, *English Literature in the Early Eighteenth Century*, 1959, p. 218.

[3] See H. T. Swedenberg, *The Theory of the Epic in England 1650–1800*, 1944.

[4] *The English Epic and its Background*, 1954, p. 473.

didactic, pastoral, and descriptive verse. It appealed as strongly to Burns, in Ayrshire, at the end of the century, as it did to Pope, at Twickenham, at the beginning. It is, says Pope, 'the most noble and spirited translation that I know in any language'; and his own *Homer* stands on the foundation laid by Dryden. The *Æneis* held the eighteenth century in thrall as a model of the heroic style, and also as a great epic poem in its own right. It became 'at once a substantive part of English literature, one of the greater English poems, and Virgil entered the eighteenth century an English citizen'.[1] The *Virgil* is Dryden's finest single achievement in twenty years of 'reviving the old of past ages' for his time. There are more dependable cribs, even in verse; and Gavin Douglas's Scots version may be, as Professor Lewis claims, 'the best possible preparation for a re-reading of the Latin'. But works of imagination

excel by their allurement and delight; by their power of attracting and detaining the attention. That book is good in vain which the reader throws away. He only is the master who keeps the mind in pleasing captivity; whose pages are perused with eagerness, and in hope of new pleasure are perused again; and whose conclusion is perceived with an eye of sorrow. . . . By his proportion of this predomination I will consent that Dryden should be tried.[2]

In the time of Dryden the translator of the classics was chiefly concerned to strengthen the ties that bound the ancients and their modern admirers and imitators. An old author was to be revived in a new medium, enriching both the language and the literature of his adoption; the sense and character of his writing were sacrosanct. Dryden approached Chaucer and Boccaccio less conservatively. Chaucer was a primitive genius, to be revised and refined in accordance with the standards of the Augustan age. His language had to be transformed:

[1] George Gordon.   [2] Johnson, op. cit. i. 454.

The Words are given up as a Post not to be defended in our Poet, because he wanted the Modern Art of Fortifying. . . . When an Ancient Word for its Sound and Significancy deserves to be reviv'd, I have that reasonable Veneration for Antiquity, to restore it. All beyond this is Superstition. Words are not like Land-marks, so sacred as never to be remov'd.

Chaucer is 'a rough Diamond, and must first be polish'd ere he shines'. Dryden is freely interpretative in modernizing him, reducing or even omitting where taste requires, and adding 'somewhat of my own where I thought my Author was deficient, and had not given his Thoughts their true Lustre, for want of Words in the Beginning of our Language'. So the Knight's story of Palamon and Arcite, exemplifying the codes of chivalry and courtly love, is retold in the terms of the Restoration theatre, with all the extravagance, inflamed rhetoric, and melodramatic action of the heroic play; Chaucer's medieval joke of a talking cock and hen in the Nun's Priest's tale is delightedly elaborated in a mock-heroic tragi-comedy.

Boccaccio set Dryden a rather different task. He is still, in 1700, 'the Standard of Purity in the *Italian* Tongue'; and Dryden may have been challenged by a complaint in the anonymous English version of the *Decameron* (1620) that justice had not yet been done to his 'sweet Stile and Elocution of Phrase'. The task here is not to refine medieval crudeness and naïveté; the gulf to be bridged is less between the old-fashioned and the modern than between economical prose narrative and baroque poetry. Dryden retells the cautionary tale of Theodore and Honoria with all the trappings of Renaissance romance, of courtly society and setting, and of supernatural horror. The story of Sigismonda and Guiscardo is reshaped as a high tragedy of passion, cruelty, violence, and grief.

Boccaccio's tale of Cymon and Iphigenia (see p. 143) gave

Dryden his chance as a poet of action, a satirist, and a dramatist interested in 'the movements and affections of the mind'. The bald account of Cymon's exciting but irresponsible efforts to get Iphigenia for himself did not satisfy Dryden: a civilized and chivalrous hero, raised by love from imbecility to sophistication, does not behave like a piratical ravisher. Dryden presents him as a man whose elevated passion accords with the miraculous and violent metamorphosis of his personality. He resembles the lovers of the heroic drama, with their immense aspiration, excess of feeling, and hectic activity. 'Stormy Cymon' is heroically aggressive and incautious and this new emphasis on daring—all for love, or the world well lost—gives Dryden opportunities in a style he loved. Rhythm, imagery, and energetic diction throw the character of the swashbuckling hero into relief. Iphigenia, too, is vitalized. In Boccaccio she is a colourless figure, the vaguely defined occasion and goal of Cymon's passion: Dryden converts her into a clearcut, fairly realistic woman in his familiar half-satiric terms—beautiful, unpredictable, and a bit comic.

Dryden transformed Boccaccio's stories. The direct, purposive Italian prose becomes a leisurely, decorated, and imaginative poetry; Boccaccio's objectivity gives place to energetic concernment. The medieval *Fables* taken together illustrate Dryden's inimitable power in argument and in the description of violence, his sense of character and situation, his love of psychological analysis, his peculiar facility in heroic-satiric writing, and (in his pictorial passages) a 'romantic' sensitiveness to atmosphere.

Wordsworth wrote to Scott on Dryden:

I admire his talents and genius highly—but his is not a poetical genius. The only qualities I can find in Dryden that are *essentially* poetical, are a certain ardour and impetuosity of mind, with an excellent ear. It may seem strange that I do not add to this, great command of language: *That* he certainly has, and of such language too, as it is most desirable that a poet should possess. . . . But it is not language that is, in the highest sense of the word, poetical, being neither of the imagination nor of the passions.[1]

Dryden's 'ardour and impetuosity of mind' are commonplaces of criticism. But although few have subscribed to Arnold's extreme view that 'Dryden and Pope are not classics of our poetry, they are classics of our prose' few have disagreed with the implications of Wordsworth's comments on Dryden's poetic diction. He is acknowledged a powerful writer, vital and often exciting, but too conspicuously the master of rhetorical 'statement' to claim a place among the best poets.

T. S. Eliot has done much to reduce the seriousness of this charge. 'The depreciation or neglect of Dryden,' he says, 'is not due to the fact that his work is not poetry, but to a prejudice that the material, the feelings, out of which he builds, is not poetic.' This defence rests on a revaluation of the argumentative, satiric, and rhetorical elements in his writing. Eliot, in affirming that Dryden is poetic just where the Romantic critics thought him prosaic, represents him as essentially a non-'romantic' poet: he

bears a curiously antithetic resemblance to Swinburne. Swinburne was also a master of words, but Swinburne's words are all suggestion and no denotation; if they suggest nothing, it is because they suggest too much. Dryden's words, on the other hand, are precise, they state immensely, but their suggestiveness is almost nothing.

From the perfection of such an elegy [on Oldham; see p. 88] we cannot detract: the lack of suggestiveness is compensated by the satisfying completeness of the statement.[2]

Dryden does not, however, fit into the category where denotation is all and connotation nothing; and critics have been

---

[1] Letter of 7 November 1805; Lockhart, *Life of Scott*, 1914, i. 433–4.
[2] *Selected Essays*, 1932, pp. 308–9, 314–15, 316.

too ready to read back into his poetry the undiluted clarity,
precision, and finality that are characteristic of some kinds of
eighteenth-century verse. It is true that he lived through an age
when the reaction against the fantastic and obscure, against
poetic ellipsis and metaphysical wit, was producing a simpler
style; and he played a main part in that reaction. But his
natural boldness would not let him rest content with a simple,
merely denotative poetic manner, and his magnificent obvious-
ness is often illusory. Indeed his delight, Johnson complains,

was in wild and daring sallies of sentiment, in the irregular and ex-
centrick violence of wit. He delighted to tread upon the brink of
meaning, where light and darkness begin to mingle; to approach the
precipice of absurdity, and hover over the abyss of unideal vacancy.[1]

Modern readers, looking back to Dryden beyond the
Romantics, are conditioned to ask for a brilliant and suggestive
novelty that he seldom offers. Professor Tillotson succinctly ex-
presses the difference between the poetic suggestion of the best
Augustans and that of the Romantics. The Augustans, he says,

knew that a reader soon scrambles on to the level of a poem, and that
when he has reached it, that level becomes his norm. . . . In *Endymion*,
everything is so exotic that, to provide a surprise, Keats almost has to
burst a blood-vessel. In Gray's *Elegy*, the even tenor of the style gives
to words like 'tinklings' the equivalent of an 'angelic strength'.[2]

Here Dryden's conception of language as the subtly chosen
dress, or final colouring, of the poet's thoughts—as opposed
to later notions of poetic language as the ultimate and inevitable expression of thought—is important. The language of
poetry was, for him, essentially a 'made' language. It is the
firm, durable groundwork of current vocabulary and idiom
that gives his diction a deceptively plain and prosaic appear-
ance. But in the occasional calculated novelty—giving a new

[1] Op. cit. i. 460.
[2] *Essays in Criticism and Research*, 1942, pp. 59–60.

(or an ancient) turn of meaning to a common word, dropping into colloquialism, recovering a word laden with venerable associations, echoing the diction of his Latin masters—Dryden's language takes on a large measure of suggestion. That the number of potentially suggestive words in his diction is small is not important. The poet who touches a plain style with subtly disposed light, shade, and colour may give a more delicate impression of richness than does one who scrapes his palette out in every paragraph. And stone is a more durable medium than plasticine.

The centrifugal force in Dryden's career was a concern for the standards, techniques, and development of his art. Critics, from Johnson on, have pointed out that there were some poetic kinds in which he was quite at ease, and others which made demands on his resources that he could not meet. But more significant is his awareness of the potentialities of the established forms of poetry, and his persistent experiment with them. His critical views were often tentative and inconsistent, but he had a constant sense of a professional responsibility to keep his art vital through trials of poetic strength and resourcefulness. The concerns and tastes of his time made heavy demands on him; but he met each one as a good craftsman, reconsidering the conventions, working out his own methods, and executing his task with originality and assurance.

Perhaps no nation ever produced a writer that enriched his language with such variety of models. To him we owe the improvement, perhaps the completion of our metre, the refinement of our language, and much of the correctness of our sentiments. By him we were taught 'sapere et fari', to think naturally and express forcibly.... What was said of Rome, adorned by Augustus, may be applied by an easy metaphor to English poetry embellished by Dryden, 'lateritiam invenit, marmoream reliquit', he found it brick, and he left it marble.[1]

[1] Johnson, op. cit. i. 469.

DRYDEN'S LIFE

1631 Born at Aldwinkle All Saints, Northamptonshire, on 9 August.

164? Elected a King's Scholar at Westminster School.

1650–4 Trinity College, Cambridge.

1659 *Heroique Stanza's* in memory of Cromwell.

1660 *Astraea Redux. A Poem on the Happy Restoration and Return of . . . Charles the Second.*

1662 Admitted a Fellow of the Royal Society.

1663 Production of Dryden's first play, *The Wild Gallant: A Comedy* (pub. 1669).

Marriage to Lady Elizabeth Howard, daughter of the Earl of Berkshire.

1665 *The Indian Emperour* (pub. 1667), Dryden's first heroic play.

The Plague: London theatres closed May 1665–December 1666.

1666 The Fire of London. Dryden writes *Annus Mirabilis* (pub. 1667) at his father-in-law's house in Wiltshire.

1667 *The Tempest*, Dryden's first adaptation of Shakespeare, written in collaboration with Davenant.

Contract with the King's Theatre to furnish three plays a year.

1668 *Of Dramatick Poesie, An Essay*, Dryden's first piece of extended literary criticism (revised 1684).

Appointed Poet Laureate in succession to Davenant.

1669 *Tyrannick Love . . . A Tragedy* (pub. 1670).

1670 *The Conquest of Granada*, in two parts; Dryden's most ambitious heroic play (pub. 1672).

1672 *Marriage A-la-Mode*, the best of Dryden's comedies (pub. 1673).

1675 *Aureng-Zebe: A Tragedy* (pub. 1676).

1677 *The State of Innocence . . . An Opera . . . in Heroique Verse* based on *Paradise Lost*. It was not acted.

All for Love: or, The World Well Lost, adapted from Shakespeare's *Antony and Cleopatra* and the richest of Dryden's plays (pub. 1678).

1678 *Mac Flecknoe*. Printed without authority, 1682.

1680 *Ovid's Epistles, Translated* (preface and two epistles by Dryden). *The Spanish Fryar* (pub. 1681).

1681 *Absalom and Achitophel. A Poem.*

1682 *The Medall. A Satyre against Sedition* (March).

The Second Part of Absalom and Achitophel, by Nahum Tate but with additions and revisions by Dryden (November).

Religio Laici or A Laymans Faith. A Poem.

1683 'Life of Plutarch' prefixed to *Plutarch's Lives, Translated.*

1684 *Miscellany Poems.*

1685 *Sylvae: or, The Second Part of Miscellany Poems* (preface and translations from Virgil, Lucretius, and Theocritus, by Dryden).

Threnodia Augustalis: A Funeral-Pindarique Poem in memory of Charles II (died 6 February).

1686 Dryden received into the Roman Church.

1687 *The Hind and the Panther. A Poem.*

A Song for St. Cecilia's Day (November).

1688 *Britannia Rediviva: A Poem on the Birth of the Prince* (the 'Old Pretender', born 10 June).

Abdication of James II.

1689 Succession of William and Mary. Dryden loses his offices of Poet Laureate and Historiographer Royal to the Whig Shadwell.

1690 *Don Sebastian . . . A Tragedy. Amphitryon . . . A Comedy.*

1691 *King Arthur . . . A Dramatick Opera.*

1692 *Cleomenes, The Spartan Heroe. A Tragedy.*

1693 *The Satires* of Juvenal and Persius, translated mainly by Dryden, with a critical 'Discourse concerning the Original and Progress of Satire'.

Examen Poeticum: Being the Third Part of Miscellany Poems (preface and translations from Ovid and Homer by Dryden).

1694 *The Annual Miscellany* (the fourth miscellany volume, with two pieces by Dryden).

Love Triumphant: A Tragi-Comedy. Dryden's last play.

1695 'A Parallel betwixt Painting and Poetry' prefixed to a translation of Du Fresnoy's *De Arte Graphica.*

1697 *The Works of Virgil*, Dryden's most sustained single work.

Alexander's Feast; or The Power of Musique. An Ode.

1700 *Fables Ancient and Modern* translated from Chaucer, Boccaccio, Homer, and Ovid, with a preface.

The Secular Masque.

Dryden dies, 1 May; buried in Westminster Abbey, 13 May.

SELECT BIBLIOGRAPHY

[On the early editions, see Hugh Macdonald, *John Dryden: A Bibliography* (Oxford, 1939).]

I. EDITIONS OF DRYDEN'S WORKS

(a) Collected Works

Works, ed. Walter Scott (London, 1808, 18 vols.; revised G. Saintsbury, 1882–93). A new collected edition is in preparation at Berkeley, California (vol. 1, 1956).

The Poems, ed. James Kinsley (Oxford, 1958, 4 vols.). Reprint of the original poems and *Fables*, Oxford Standard Authors (London, 1962).

Essays, ed. W. P. Ker (Oxford, 1900, 2 vols.); ed. George Watson (London, 1962, 2 vols.).

Letters, ed. C. E. Ward (Chapel Hill, North Carolina, 1942).

(b) Selections and Separate Works

Poetry, prose and plays, ed. Douglas Grant (London, 1952).

Marriage A-la-Mode, ed. J. R. Sutherland (London, 1934).

All for Love in *Five Restoration Tragedies*, ed. B. Dobrée (London, 1928).

Absalom and Achitophel, ed. J. and H. Kinsley (Oxford, 1961).

The Works of Virgil, with intro. by J. Kinsley (Oxford, 1961).

II. BIOGRAPHY AND CRITICISM

(a) Books

Samuel Johnson, in *Lives of the English Poets* (London, 1779–81).

Walter Scott, in *Works of Dryden* (London, 1808).

M. Van Doren, *The Poetry of Dryden* (New York, 1920; 1946, with the title *Dryden: A Study of his Poetry*).

L. I. Bredvold, *The Intellectual Milieu of John Dryden* (Ann Arbor, 1934).

J. M. Osborn, *Dryden: Some Biographical Facts and Problems* (New York, 1940).

D. Nichol Smith, *Dryden* (Cambridge, 1950).

W. Frost, *Dryden and the Art of Translation* (New Haven, 1955).
George Watson, in *The Literary Critics* (London, 1962).

(*b*) *Articles*

T. S. Eliot, 'Homage to John Dryden', 1924, in *Selected Essays* (London, 1932).

C. S. Lewis, 'Shelley, Dryden, and Mr. Eliot', in *Rehabilitations* (London, 1934).

NOTE ON THE TEXT

The text of the poems is reprinted from the complete collection of Dryden's poetry edited by James Kinsley for the Oxford English Texts (Clarendon Press, 1958). The line numbers printed in square brackets refer to that edition.

Prologue to The Assignation

Performed October 1672. Published 1673

PROLOGUES, like Bells to Churches, toul you in
With Chimeing Verse; till the dull Playes begin:
With this sad difference though, of Pit and Pue;
You damn the *Poet*, but the *Priest* damns you.
But Priests can treat you at your own expence: 5
And, gravely, call you Fooles, without offence.
Poets, poor Devils, have ne'r your Folly shown
But, to their cost, you prov'd it was their own.
For, when a Fop's presented on the Stage,
Straight all the Coxcombs in the Town ingage: 10
For his deliverance, and revenge they joyn:
And grunt, like Hogs, about their Captive Swine.
Your Poets daily split upon this shelfe:
You must have Fooles, yet none will have himself.
Or, if in kindness, you that leave would give,   15
No man could write you at that rate you live:
For some of you grow Fops with so much haste,⎫
Riot in nonsense, and commit such waste,   ⎬
'Twould Ruine Poets should they spend so fast.⎭
He who made this, observ'd what Farces hit,   20
And durst not disoblige you now with wit.
But, Gentlemen, you overdo the Mode:
You must have Fooles out of the common Rode.
Th' unnatural strain'd Buffoon is onely taking:
No Fop can please you now of Gods own making.   25
Pardon our Poet if he speaks his Mind,
You come to Plays with your own Follies lin'd:

Small Fooles fall on you, like small showers, in vain:
You own oyl'd Coates keep out all common raine.
You must have Mamamouchi, such a Fop   30
As would appear a Monster in a Shop:
Hee'l fill your Pit and Boxes to the brim,
Where, Ram'd in Crowds, you see your selves in him.
Sure there's some spell our Poet never knew,
In hullibabilah da, and Chu, chu, chu.   35
But Marabarah sahem most did touch you,
That is: Oh how we love the Mamamouchi!
Grimace and habit sent you pleas'd away:
You damn'd the Poet, and cry'd up the Play.
    This thought had made our Author more uneasie,   40
But that he hopes I'm Fool enough to please ye:
But here's my griefe; though Nature joyn'd with art,
Have cut me out to act a Fooling Part;
Yet, to your praise, the few wits here will say,
'Twas imitating you taught *Haynes* to Play.   45

Epilogue to The Wild Gallant *Reviv'd*

Performed February 1663. Revived 1667. Published 1669

Oꜰ all Dramatique Writing, Comick Wit,
As 'tis the best, so 'tis most hard to hit.
For it lies all in level to the eye,
Where all may judge, and each defect may spye.
Humour is that which every day we meet,   5
And therefore known as every publick street;
In which, if e'r the Poet go astray
You all can point, 'twas there he lost his way.
But, What's so common, to make pleasant too,

Is more than any wit can alwayes do.   10
For 'tis, like *Turkes*, with Hen and Rice to treat;
To make regallio's out of common meat.
But, in your Diet you grow Salvages:
Nothing but Humane flesh your taste can please:
And, as their Feasts with slaughter'd slaves began,   15
So you, at each new Play, must have a Man.
Hither you come, as to see Prizes fought;
If no Blood's drawn, you cry the Prize is naught.
But fooles grow wary now; and when they see
A Poet eyeing round the Company,   20
Straight each man for himself begins to doubt;
They shrink like Seamen when a Press comes out.
Few of 'em will be found for Publick use,
Except you charge an Oph upon each house,
Like the Traind-Bands, and every man ingage   25
For a sufficient Foole to serve the Stage.
And, when with much adoe you get him there,
Where he in all his glory shou'd appear,
Your Poets make him such rare things to say,
That he's more wit than any Man ith' Play.   30
But of so ill a mingle with the rest,
As when a Parrat's taught to break a jeast.
Thus aiming to be fine, they make a show
As tawdry Squires in Country Churches do.
Things well consider'd, 'tis so hard to make   35
A Comedy, which should the knowing take:
That our dull Poet, in despair to please,
Does humbly beg by me his writ of ease.
'Tis a Land-tax which he's too poor to pay;
You, therefore, must some other impost lay.   40
Would you but change for serious Plot and Verse
This mottley garniture of Fool and Farce,

Nor scorn a Mode, because 'tis taught at home,
Which does, like Vests, our Gravity become;
Our Poet yields you should this Play refuse,   45
As Tradesmen, by the change of fashions, lose
With some content their fripperies of *France*,
In hope it may their staple Trade advance.

Prologue to The Second Part of The Conquest of Granada

Performed December–January 1670–1. Published 1672

THEY who write Ill, and they who ne'r durst write,
Turn Critiques, out of meer Revenge and Spight:
A *Play-house* gives 'em Fame; and up there starts,
From a mean Fifth-rate Wit, a Man of Parts.
(So Common Faces on the Stage appear: 5
We take 'em in; and they turn Beauties here.)
Our Authour fears those Critiques as his Fate:
And those he Fears, by consequence, must Hate.
For they the Trafficque of all Wit, invade;
As Scriv'ners draw away the Bankers Trade.   10
Howe're, the Poet's safe enough to day:
They cannot censure an unfinish'd Play.
But, as when Vizard Masque appears in Pit,
Straight, every man who thinks himself a Wit,
Perks up; and, managing his Comb, with grace,   15
With his white Wigg sets off his Nut-brown Face:
That done, bears up to th' prize, and views each Limb,
To know her by her Rigging and her Trimm:
Then, the whole noise of Fopps to wagers go,
Pox on her, 't must be she; and *Damm'ee* no: 20

Just so I Prophecy, these Wits to day,
Will blindly guess at our imperfect Play:
With what new Plots our Second Part is fill'd;
Who must be kept alive, and who be kill'd.
And as those Vizard Masques maintain that Fashion,   25
To sooth and tickle sweet Imagination:
So, our dull Poet keeps you on with Masquing;
To make you think there's something worth your asking:
But when 'tis shown, that which does now delight you,
Will prove a Dowdy, with a Face to fright you.   30

Prologue to the University of Oxford

Written by 1676. *Miscellany Poems* (1684)

THO' Actors cannot much of Learning boast,
Of all who want it, we admire it most.
We love the Praises of a Learned Pit,
As we remotely are ally'd to Wit.
We speak our Poets Wit, and Trade in Ore,   5
Like those who touch upon the Golden Shore:
Betwixt our Judges can distinction make,
Discern how much, and why, our Poems take.
Mark if the Fools, or Men of Sence, rejoyce,
Whether th' Applause be only Sound or Voice.   10
When our Fop Gallants, or our City Folly
Clap over-loud, it makes us melancholy:
We doubt that Scene which does their wonder raise,
And, for their ignorance contemn their Praise.
Judge then, if We who Act, and They who Write,   15
Shou'd not be proud of giving You delight.
London likes grossly, but this nicer Pit
Examines, Fathoms all the depths of Wit:

The ready Finger lays on every Blot,
Knows what shou'd justly please, and what shou'd not.   20
Nature her self lies open to your view,
You judge by Her what draught of Her is true,
Where out lines false, and Colours seem too faint,
Where Bunglers dawb, and where True Poets Paint.
But by the Sacred Genius of this Place,   25
By every Muse, by each Domestick Grace,
Be kind to Wit, which but endeavours well,
And, where you judge, presumes not to excel.
Our Poets hither for Adoption come,
As Nations su'd to be made Free of *Rome*.   30
Not in the suffragating Tribes to stand,
But in your utmost, last, Provincial Band.
If His Ambition may those Hopes pursue,
Who with Religion loves Your Arts and You,
Oxford to Him a dearer Name shall be,   35
Than His own Mother University.
Thebes did His Green, unknowing Youth ingage,
He chuses *Athens* in His Riper Age.

Prologue to the Dutchess on her Return from Scotland

Written and published May 1682

WHEN Factious Rage to cruel Exile, drove
The Queen of Beauty, and the Court of Love;
The Muses Droop'd, with their forsaken Arts,
And the sad *Cupids* broke their useless Darts.
Our fruitfull Plains to Wilds and Desarts turn'd,   5

Like *Edens* Face when banish'd Man it mourn'd:
Love was no more when Loyalty was gone,
The great Supporter of his Awfull Throne.
Love cou'd no longer after Beauty stay,
But wander'd Northward to the verge of day,   10
As if the Sun and He had lost their way.
But now th' Illustrious Nymph return'd again,
Brings every Grace triumphant in her Train:
The wondring *Nereids*, though they rais'd no storm,
Foreslow'd her passage to behold her form: 15
Some cry'd a *Venus*, some a *Thetis* past:
But this was not so fair, nor that so chast.
Far from her sight flew Faction, Strife and Pride:
And Envy did but look on her, and dy'd.
What e'er we suffer'd from our sullen Fate,   20
Her sight is purchas'd at an easy rate:
Three gloomy Years against this day were set:
But this one mighty Sum has clear'd the Debt.
Like *Joseph*'s Dream, but with a better doom;
The Famine past, the Plenty still to come.   25
For Her the weeping Heav'ns become serene,
For Her the Ground is clad in cheerfull green:
For Her the Nightingales are taught to sing,
And Nature has for her delay'd the Spring.
The Muse resumes her long-forgotten Lays,   30
And Love, restor'd, his Ancient Realm surveys;
Recalls our Beauties, and revives our Plays.
His Wast Dominions peoples once again,
And from Her presence dates his Second Reign.
But awfull Charms on her fair Forehead sit,   35
Dispensing what she never will admit.
Pleasing, yet cold, like *Cynthia*'s silver Beam,
The Peoples Wonder, and the Poets Theam.

Distemper'd Zeal, Sedition, canker'd Hate,
No more shall vex the Church, and tear the State;   40
No more shall Faction civil Discords move,
Or onely discords of too tender love:
Discord like that of Musicks various parts,
Discord that makes the harmony of Hearts,
Discord that onely this dispute shall bring,   45
Who best shall love the Duke, and serve the King.

Portraits from Absalom and Achitophel

Published November 1681

OF these the false *Achitophel* was first: [150]
A Name to all succeeding Ages Curst.
For close Designs, and crooked Counsels fit;
Sagacious, Bold, and Turbulent of wit:
Restless, unfixt in Principles and Place;   5
In Power unpleas'd, impatient of Disgrace.
A fiery Soul, which working out its way,⎫
Fretted the Pigmy Body to decay: ⎬
And o'r inform'd the Tenement of Clay. ⎭
A daring Pilot in extremity;   10
Pleas'd with the Danger, when the Waves went high
He sought the Storms; but for a Calm unfit,
Would Steer too nigh the Sands, to boast his Wit.
Great Wits are sure to Madness near ally'd;
And thin Partitions do their Bounds divide: 15
Else, why should he, with Wealth and Honour blest,
Refuse his Age the needful hours of Rest?
Punish a Body which he coud not please;
Bankrupt of Life, yet Prodigal of Ease?

And all to leave, what with his Toyl he won,   20
To that unfeather'd, two Leg'd thing, a Son: [170]
Got, while his Soul did hudled Notions try;
And born a shapeless Lump, like Anarchy.
In Friendship False, Implacable in Hate:
Resolv'd to Ruine or to Rule the State.   25
To Compass this the Triple Bond he broke; ⎫
The Pillars of the publick Safety shook: ⎬
And fitted *Israel* for a Foreign Yoke.   ⎭
Then, seiz'd with Fear, yet still affecting Fame,
Usurp'd a Patriott's All-attoning Name.   30
So easie still it proves in Factious Times,
With publick Zeal to cancel private Crimes:
How safe is Treason, and how sacred ill,
Where none can sin against the Peoples Will:
Where Crouds can wink; and no offence be known,   35
Since in anothers guilt they find their own.
Yet, Fame deserv'd, no Enemy can grudge;
The Statesman we abhor, but praise the Judge.
In *Israels* Courts ne'r sat an *Abbethdin*
With more discerning Eyes, or Hands more clean: 40
Unbrib'd, unsought, the Wretched to redress;   [190]
Swift of Dispatch, and easie of Access.
Oh, had he been content to serve the Crown,
With vertues only proper to the Gown;
Or, had the rankness of the Soyl been freed   45
From Cockle, that opprest the Noble seed:
David, for him his tunefull Harp had strung,
And Heaven had wanted one Immortal song.
But wilde Ambition loves to slide, not stand;
And Fortunes Ice prefers to Vertues Land: 50
Achitophel, grown weary to possess
A lawfull Fame, and lazy Happiness;

Disdain'd the Golden fruit to gather free,
And lent the Croud his Arm to shake the Tree.
Now, manifest of Crimes, contriv'd long since,   55
He stood at bold Defiance with his Prince:
Held up the Buckler of the Peoples Cause,
Against the Crown; and sculk'd behind the Laws.
The wish'd occasion of the Plot he takes,
Some Circumstances finds, but more he makes.   60
By buzzing Emissaries, fills the ears   [210]
Of listning Crowds, with Jealosies and Fears
Of Arbitrary Counsels brought to light,
And proves the King himself a *Jebusite*:
Weak Arguments! which yet he knew full well,   65
Were strong with People easie to Rebell.
For, govern'd by the *Moon*, the giddy *Jews*
Tread the same track when she the Prime renews:
And once in twenty Years, their Scribes Record,
By natural Instinct they change their Lord.   70

★   ★   ★   ★

Some of their Chiefs were Princes of the Land:
In the first Rank of these did *Zimri* stand:
A man so various, that he seem'd to be
Not one, but all Mankinds Epitome.
Stiff in Opinions, always in the wrong;   75
Was every thing by starts, and nothing long:
But, in the course of one revolving Moon,
Was Chymist, Fidler, States-Man, and Buffoon: [550]
Then all for Women, Painting, Rhiming, Drinking;
Besides ten thousand freaks that dy'd in thinking.   80
Blest Madman, who coud every hour employ,
With something New to wish, or to enjoy!

Rayling and praising were his usual Theams;
And both (to shew his Judgment) in Extreams:
So over Violent, or over Civil,   85
That every man, with him, was God or Devil.
In squandring Wealth was his peculiar Art:
Nothing went unrewarded, but Desert.
Begger'd by Fools, whom still he found too late:
He had his Jest, and they had his Estate.   90
He laught himself from Court, then sought Relief
By forming Parties, but coud ne're be Chief:
For, spight of him, the weight of Business fell
On *Absalom* and wise *Achitophel*:
Thus, wicked but in will, of means bereft,   95
He left not Faction, but of that was left.

   Titles and Names 'twere tedious to Reherse
Of Lords, below the Dignity of Verse.   [570]
Wits, warriors, Common-wealthsmen, were the best:
Kind Husbands and meer Nobles all the rest.   100
And, therefore in the name of Dulness, be
The well hung *Balaam* and cold *Caleb* free.
And Canting *Nadab* let Oblivion damn,
Who made new porridge for the Paschal Lamb.
Let Friendships holy band some Names assure: 105
Some their own Worth, and some let Scorn secure.
Nor shall the Rascall Rabble here have Place,
Whom Kings no Titles gave, and God no Grace:
Not Bull-fac'd *Jonas*, who could Statutes draw
To mean Rebellion, and make Treason Law.   110
But he, tho bad, is follow'd by a worse,
The wretch, who Heavens Annointed dar'd to Curse.
Shimei, whose Youth did early Promise bring
Of Zeal to God, and Hatred to his King;
Did wisely from Expensive Sins refrain,   115

And never broke the Sabbath, but for Gain:
Nor ever was he known an Oath to vent,
Or Curse unless against the Government.   [590]
Thus, heaping Wealth, by the most ready way
Among the *Jews*, which was to Cheat and Pray;   120
The City, to reward his pious Hate
Against his Master, chose him Magistrate:
His Hand a Vare of Justice did uphold;
His Neck was loaded with a Chain of Gold.
During his Office, Treason was no Crime.   125
The Sons of *Belial* had a glorious Time:
For *Shimei*, though not prodigal of pelf,
Yet lov'd his wicked Neighbour as himself:
When two or three were gather'd to declaim ⎫
Against the Monarch of *Jerusalem*,   ⎬ 130
Shimei was always in the midst of them.   ⎭
And, if they Curst the King when he was by,
Woud rather Curse, than break good Company.
If any durst his Factious Friends accuse,
He pact a Jury of dissenting *Jews*:   135
Whose fellow-feeling, in the godly Cause,
Woud free the suffring Saint from Humane Laws.
For Laws are only made to Punish those,   [610]
Who serve the King, and to protect his Foes.
If any leisure time he had from Power,   140
(Because 'tis Sin to misimploy an hour;)
His business was, by Writing, to Persuade,
That Kings were Useless, and a Clog to Trade:
And, that his noble Stile he might refine,
No *Rechabite* more shund the fumes of Wine.   145
Chast were his Cellars, and his Shrieval Board
The Grossness of a City Feast abhor'd:
His Cooks, with long disuse, their Trade forgot;

Cool was his Kitchen, tho his Brains were hot.
Such frugal Vertue Malice may accuse,   150
But sure 'twas necessary to the *Jews*:
For Towns once burnt, such Magistrates require
As dare not tempt Gods Providence by fire.
With Spiritual food he fed his Servants well,
But free from flesh, that made the *Jews* Rebel: 155
And *Moses*'s Laws he held in more account,
For forty days of Fasting in the Mount.

    To speak the rest, who better are forgot,   [630]
Would tyre a well breath'd Witness of the Plot:
Yet, *Corah*, thou shalt from Oblivion pass;   160
Erect thy self thou Monumental Brass:
High as the Serpent of thy mettall made,
While Nations stand secure beneath thy shade.
What tho his Birth were base, yet Comets rise
From Earthy Vapours ere they shine in Skies.   165
Prodigious Actions may as well be done
By Weavers issue, as by Princes Son.
This Arch-Attestor for the Publick Good,
By that one Deed Enobles all his Bloud.
Who ever ask'd the Witnesses high race,   170
Whose Oath with Martyrdom did *Stephen* grace?
Ours was a *Levite*, and as times went then,
His Tribe were Godalmightys Gentlemen.
Sunk were his Eyes, his Voyce was harsh and loud,
Sure signs he neither Cholerick was, nor Proud: 175
His long Chin prov'd his Wit; his Saintlike Grace
A Church Vermilion, and a *Moses*'s Face;
His Memory, miraculously great,   [650]
Could Plots, exceeding mans belief, repeat;
Which, therefore cannot be accounted Lies,   180
For humane Wit could never such devise.

Some future Truths are mingled in his Book;
But, where the witness faild, the Prophet Spoke:
Some things like Visionary flights appear;
The Spirit caught him up, the Lord knows where: 185
And gave him his *Rabinical* degree
Unknown to Foreign University.
His Judgment yet his Memory did excel;
Which peic'd his wondrous Evidence so well:
And suited to the temper of the times;   190
Then groaning under *Jebusitick* Crimes.
Let *Israels* foes suspect his heav'nly call,
And rashly judge his Writ Apocryphal;
Our Laws for such affronts have forfeits made:
He takes his life, who takes away his trade.   195
Were I my self in witness *Corahs* place,
The wretch who did me such a dire disgrace,
Should whet my memory, though once forgot,   [670]
To make him an Appendix of my Plot.
His Zeal to heav'n, made him his Prince despise,   200
And load his person with indignities:
But Zeal peculiar priviledg affords;
Indulging latitude to deeds and words.
And *Corah* might for *Agag*'s murther call,
In terms as course as *Samuel* us'd to *Saul*.   205
What others in his Evidence did Joyn,
(The best that could be had for love or coyn,)
In *Corah*'s own predicament will fall:
For *witness* is a Common Name to all.

From The Medall. A Satyre Against Sedition

Published March 1682

Of all our Antick Sights, and Pageantry
Which *English* Ideots run in crowds to see,
The *Polish Medall* bears the prize alone:
A Monster, more the Favourite of the Town
Than either Fayrs or Theatres have shown.   5
Never did Art so well with Nature strive;
Nor ever Idol seem'd so much alive:
So like the Man; so golden to the sight,
So base within, so counterfeit and light.
One side is fill'd with Title and with Face;   10
And, lest the King shou'd want a regal Place,
On the reverse, a Tow'r the Town surveys;
O'er which our mounting Sun his beams displays.
The Word, pronounc'd aloud by Shrieval voice,
Lætamur, which, in *Polish*, is *rejoyce*.   15
The Day, Month, Year, to the great Act are join'd:
And a new Canting Holiday design'd.
Five daies he sate, for every cast and look;
Four more than God to finish *Adam* took.
But who can tell what Essence Angels are,   20
Or how long Heav'n was making *Lucifer*?
Oh, cou'd the Style that copy'd every grace,
And plough'd such furrows for an Eunuch face,
Cou'd it have form'd his ever-changing Will,
The various Piece had tir'd the Graver's Skill!   25
A Martial Heroe first, with early care,
Blown, like a Pigmee by the Winds, to war.

A beardless Chief, a Rebel, e'r a Man:
(So young his hatred to his Prince began.)
Next this, (How wildly will Ambition steer!)   30
A Vermin, wriggling in th' Usurper's Ear.
Bart'ring his venal wit for sums of gold
He cast himself into the Saint-like mould;
Groan'd, sigh'd and pray'd, while Godliness was gain;
The lowdest Bagpipe of the squeaking Train.   35
But, as 'tis hard to cheat a Juggler's Eyes,
His open lewdness he cou'd ne'er disguise.
There split the Saint: for Hypocritique Zeal
Allows no Sins but those it can conceal.
Whoring to Scandal gives too large a scope: 40
Saints must not trade; but they may interlope.
Th' ungodly Principle was all the same;
But a gross Cheat betrays his Partner's Game.
Besides, their pace was formal, grave and slack:
His nimble Wit outran the heavy Pack.   45
Yet still he found his Fortune at a stay;
Whole droves of Blockheads choaking up his way;
They took, but not rewarded, his advice;
Villain and Wit exact a double price.
Pow'r was his aym: but, thrown from that pretence,   50
The Wretch turn'd loyal in his own defence;
And Malice reconcil'd him to his Prince.
Him, in the anguish of his Soul he serv'd;
Rewarded faster still than he deserv'd,
Behold him now exalted into trust;   55
His Counsel's oft convenient, seldom just.
Ev'n in the most sincere advice he gave
He had a grudging still to be a Knave.
The Frauds he learnt in his Fanatique years
Made him uneasy in his lawfull gears.   60

At best as little honest as he cou'd:
And, like white Witches, mischievously good.
To his first byass, longingly he leans;
And *rather* wou'd be great by wicked means.
Thus, fram'd for ill, he loos'd our Triple hold;   65
(Advice unsafe, precipitous, and bold.)
From hence those tears! that *Ilium* of our woe!
Who helps a pow'rfull Friend, fore-arms a Foe.
What wonder if the Waves prevail so far
When He cut down the Banks that made the bar?   70
Seas follow but their Nature to invade;
But He by Art our native Strength betray'd.
So *Sampson* to his Foe his force confest;
And, to be shorn, lay slumb'ring on her breast.
But, when this fatal Counsel, found too late,   75
Expos'd its Authour to the publique hate;
When his just Sovereign, by no impious way,
Cou'd be seduc'd to Arbitrary sway;
Forsaken of that hope, he shifts the sayle;
Drives down the Current with a pop'lar gale;   80
And shews the Fiend confess'd, without a vaile.
He preaches to the Crowd, that Pow'r is lent,
But not convey'd to Kingly Government;
That Claimes successive bear no binding force;
That Coronation Oaths are things of course;   85
Maintains the Multitude can never err;
And sets the People in the Papal Chair.
The reason's obvious; *Int'rest never lyes;*   ⎫
The most have still their Int'rest in their eyes; ⎬
The pow'r is always theirs, and pow'r is ever wise.⎭   90
Almighty Crowd, thou shorten'st all dispute;
Pow'r is thy Essence; Wit thy Attribute!
Nor Faith nor Reason make thee at a stay,

Thou leapst o'r all eternal truths, in thy *Pindarique* way!
Athens, no doubt, did righteously decide, 95
When *Phocion* and when *Socrates* were try'd:
As righteously they did those dooms repent;
Still they were wise, what ever way they went.
Crowds err not, though to both extremes they run;
To kill the Father, and recall the Son. 100
Some think the Fools were most, as times went then;
But now the World's o'r stock'd with prudent men.
The common Cry is ev'n Religion's Test;
The *Turk*'s is, at *Constantinople*, best;
Idols in *India*, Popery at *Rome*; 105
And our own Worship onely true at home.
And true, but for the time, 'tis hard to know
How long we please it shall continue so.
This side to day, and that to morrow burns;
So all are God-a'mighties in their turns. 110
A Tempting Doctrine, plausible and new:
What Fools our Fathers were, if this be true!
Who, to destroy the seeds of Civil War,
Inherent right in Monarchs did declare:
And, that a lawfull Pow'r might never cease, 115
Secur'd Succession, to secure our Peace.
Thus, Property and Sovereign Sway, at last
In equal Balances were justly cast:
But this new *Jehu* spurs the hot mouth'd horse;
Instructs the Beast to know his native force; 120
To take the Bit between his teeth and fly
To the next headlong Steep of Anarchy.
Too happy *England*, if our good we knew;
Wou'd we possess the freedom we pursue!
The lavish Government can give no more: 125
Yet we repine; and plenty makes us poor.

God try'd us once; our Rebel-fathers fought;
He glutted 'em with all the pow'r they sought:
Till, master'd by their own usurping Brave,
The free-born Subject sunk into a Slave.   130
We loath our Manna, and we long for Quails;
Ah, what is man, when his own wish prevails!
How rash, how swift to plunge himself in ill;
Proud of his Pow'r, and boundless in his Will!
That Kings can doe no wrong we must believe: 135
None can they doe, and must they all receive?
Help Heaven! or sadly we shall see an hour,
When neither wrong nor right are in their pow'r!
Already they have lost their best defence,
The benefit of Laws, which they dispence.   140
No justice to their righteous Cause allow'd;
But baffled by an Arbitrary Crowd.
And Medalls grav'd, their Conquest to record,
The Stamp and Coyn of their adopted Lord.

*   *   *   *

Such impious Axiomes foolishly they show;   145
For, in some Soyles Republiques will not grow:
Our Temp'rate Isle will no extremes sustain,
Of pop'lar Sway, or Arbitrary Reign:
But slides between them both into the best;   [250]
Secure in freedom, in a Monarch blest.   150
And though the Clymate, vex't with various Winds,
Works through our yielding Bodies, on our Minds,
The wholsome Tempest purges what it breeds;
To recommend the Calmness that succeeds.
  But thou, the Pander of the Peoples hearts,   155
(O Crooked Soul, and Serpentine in Arts,)
Whose blandishments a Loyal Land have whor'd,

And broke the Bonds she plighted to her Lord;
What Curses on thy blasted Name will fall!
Which Age to Age their Legacy shall call;   160
For all must curse the Woes that must descend on all.
Religion thou hast none: thy *Mercury*
Has pass'd through every Sect, or theirs through Thee.
But what thou giv'st, that Venom still remains;
And the pox'd Nation feels Thee in their Brains.   165
What else inspires the Tongues, and swells the Breasts
Of all thy bellowing Renegado Priests,
That preach up Thee for God; dispence thy Laws;
And with thy Stumm ferment their fainting Cause?   [270]
Fresh Fumes of Madness raise; and toile and sweat   170
To make the formidable Cripple great.
Yet, shou'd thy Crimes succeed, shou'd lawless Pow'r
Compass those Ends thy greedy Hopes devour,
Thy Canting Friends thy Mortal Foes wou'd be;
Thy God and Theirs will never long agree.   175
For thine, (if thou hast any,) must be one
That lets the World and Humane-kind alone:
A jolly God, that passes hours too well
To promise Heav'n, or threaten us with Hell.
That unconcern'd can at Rebellion sit;   180
And Wink at Crimes he did himself commit.
A Tyrant theirs; the Heav'n their Priesthood paints
A Conventicle of gloomy sullen Saints;
A Heav'n, like *Bedlam*, slovenly and sad;
Fore-doom'd for Souls, with false Religion, mad.   185
  Without a Vision Poets can fore-show
What all but Fools, by common Sense may know:
If true Succession from our Isle shou'd fail,
And Crowds profane, with impious Arms prevail,   [290]
Not Thou, nor those thy Factious Arts ingage   190

Shall reap that Harvest of Rebellious Rage,
With which thou flatter'st thy decrepit Age.
The swelling Poyson of the sev'ral Sects,
Which wanting vent, the Nations Health infects
Shall burst its Bag; and fighting out their way   195
The various Venoms on each other prey.
The *Presbyter*, puft up with spiritual Pride,
Shall on the Necks of the lewd Nobles ride:
His Brethren damn, the Civil Pow'r defy;
And parcel out Republique Prelacy.   200
But short shall be his Reign: his rigid Yoke
And Tyrant Pow'r will puny Sects provoke;
And Frogs and Toads, and all the Tadpole Train
Will croak to Heav'n for help, from this devouring Crane.
The Cut-throat Sword and clamorous Gown shall jar, 205
In shareing their ill-gotten Spoiles of War:
Chiefs shall be grudg'd the part which they pretend;
Lords envy Lords, and Friends with every Friend
About their impious Merit shall contend.   [310]
The surly Commons shall respect deny;   210
And justle Peerage out with Property.
Their Gen'ral either shall his Trust betray,
And force the Crowd to Arbitrary sway;
Or they suspecting his ambitious Aym,
In hate of Kings shall cast anew the Frame;   215
And thrust out *Collatine* that bore their Name.

   Thus inborn Broyles the Factions wou'd ingage;
Or Wars of Exil'd Heirs, or Foreign Rage,
Till halting Vengeance overtook our Age:
And our wild Labours, wearied into Rest,   220
Reclin'd us on a rightfull Monarch's Breast.

Mac Flecknoe

Written by 1678. Pirated edition 1682; published by Dryden 1684

ALL humane things are subject to decay,
And, when Fate summons, Monarchs must obey:
This *Fleckno* found, who, like *Augustus*, young
Was call'd to Empire, and had govern'd long:
In Prose and Verse, was own'd, without dispute   5
Through all the Realms of *Non-sense*, absolute.
This aged Prince now flourishing in Peace,
And blest with issue of a large increase,
Worn out with business, did at length debate
To settle the succession of the State: 10
And pond'ring which of all his Sons was fit
To Reign, and wage immortal War with Wit;
Cry'd, 'tis resolv'd; for Nature pleads that He
Should onely rule, who most resembles me:
Sh—— alone my perfect image bears,   15
Mature in dullness from his tender years.
Sh—— alone, of all my Sons, is he
Who stands confirm'd in full stupidity.
The rest to some faint meaning make pretence,
But *Sh*—— never deviates into sense.   20
Some Beams of Wit on other souls may fall,
Strike through and make a lucid intervall;
But *Sh*——'s genuine night admits no ray,
His rising Fogs prevail upon the Day:
Besides his goodly Fabrick fills the eye,   25
And seems design'd for thoughtless Majesty:
Thoughtless as Monarch Oakes, that shade the plain,
And, spread in solemn state, supinely reign.
Heywood and *Shirley* were but Types of thee,

Thou last great Prophet of Tautology: 30
Even I, a dunce of more renown than they,
Was sent before but to prepare thy way;
And coursly clad in *Norwich* Drugget came
To teach the Nations in thy greater name.
My warbling Lute, the Lute I whilom strung   35
When to King *John* of *Portugal* I sung,
Was but the prelude to that glorious day,
When thou on silver *Thames* did'st cut thy way,
With well tim'd Oars before the Royal Barge,
Swell'd with the Pride of thy Celestial charge;   40
And big with Hymn, Commander of an Host,
The like was ne'er in *Epsom* Blankets tost.
Methinks I see the new *Arion* Sail,
The Lute still trembling underneath thy nail.
At thy well sharpned thumb from Shore to Shore   45
The Treble squeaks for fear, the Bases roar:
Echoes from *Pissing-Ally*, *Sh*—— call,
And *Sh*—— they resound from *A*—— *Hall*.
About thy boat the little Fishes throng,
As at the Morning Toast, that Floats along.   50
Sometimes as Prince of thy Harmonious band
Thou weild'st thy **P**apers in thy threshing hand.
St. *Andre*'s feet ne'er kept more equal time,
Not ev'n the feet of thy own *Psyche*'s rhime:
Though they in number as in sense excell;   55
So just, so like tautology they fell,
That, pale with envy, *Singleton* forswore ⎞
The Lute and Sword which he in Triumph bore, ⎬
And vow'd he ne'er would act *Villerius* more. ⎠
Here stopt the good old *Syre*; and wept for joy   60
In silent raptures of the hopefull boy.
All arguments, but most his Plays, perswade,

That for anointed dullness he was made.
   Close to the Walls which fair *Augusta* bind,
(The fair *Augusta* much to fears inclin'd)   65
An ancient fabrick, rais'd t'inform the sight,
There stood of yore, and *Barbican* it hight:
A watch Tower once; but now, so Fate ordains,
Of all the Pile an empty name remains.
From its old Ruins Brothel-houses rise,   70
Scenes of lewd loves, and of polluted joys.
Where their vast Courts the Mother-Strumpets keep,
And, undisturb'd by Watch, in silence sleep.
Near these a Nursery erects its head,
Where Queens are form'd, and future Hero's bred;   75
Where unfledg'd Actors learn to laugh and cry,
Where infant Punks their tender Voices try,
And little *Maximins* the Gods defy.
Great *Fletcher* never treads in Buskins here,
Nor greater *Johnson* dares in Socks appear.   80
But gentle *Simkin* just reception finds
Amidst this Monument of vanisht minds:
Pure Clinches, the suburbian Muse affords;
And *Panton* waging harmless War with words.
Here *Fleckno*, as a place to Fame well known,   85
Ambitiously design'd his *Sh*——'s Throne.
For ancient *Decker* prophesi'd long since,
That in this Pile should Reign a mighty Prince,
Born for a scourge of Wit, and flayle of Sense:
To whom true dulness should some *Psyches* owe,   90
But Worlds of *Misers* from his pen should flow;
Humorists and *Hypocrites* it should produce,
Whole *Raymond* families, and Tribes of *Bruce*.
   Now Empress *Fame* had publisht the Renown
Of *Sh*——'s Coronation through the Town.   95

Rows'd by report of Fame, the Nations meet,
From near *Bun-Hill*, and distant *Watling-street*.
No *Persian* Carpets spread th' Imperial way,
But scatter'd Limbs of mangled Poets lay:
From dusty shops neglected Authors come,   100
Martyrs of Pies, and Reliques of the Bum.
Much *Heywood*, *Shirly*, *Ogleby* there lay,
But loads of *Sh——* almost choakt the way.
Bilk't *Stationers* for Yeomen stood prepar'd,
And *H——* was Captain of the Guard.   105
The hoary Prince in Majesty appear'd,
High on a Throne of his own Labours rear'd.
At his right hand our young *Ascanius* sate
Rome's other hope, and pillar of the State.
His Brows thick fogs, instead of glories, grace,   110
And lambent dullness plaid arround his face.
As *Hannibal* did to the Altars come,
Sworn by his *Syre* a mortal Foe to *Rome*;
So *Sh——* swore, nor should his Vow bee vain,
That he till Death true dullness would maintain;   115
And in his father's Right, and Realms defence,
Ne'er to have peace with Wit, nor truce with Sense.
The King himself the sacred Unction made,
As King by Office, and as Priest by Trade:
In his sinister hand, instead of Ball,   120
He plac'd a mighty Mug of potent Ale;
Love's Kingdom to his right he did convey,
At once his Sceptre and his rule of Sway;
Whose righteous Lore the Prince had practis'd young,
And from whose Loyns recorded *Psyche* sprung.   125
His Temples last with Poppies were o'erspread,
That nodding seem'd to consecrate his head:
Just at that point of time, if Fame not lye,

On his left hand twelve reverend *Owls* did fly.
So *Romulus*, 'tis sung, by *Tyber's Brook*,   130
Presage of Sway from twice six Vultures took.
Th' admiring throng loud acclamations make,
And Omens of his future Empire take.
The *Syre* then shook the honours of his head,
And from his brows damps of oblivion shed   135
Full on the filial dullness: long he stood,   ⎫
Repelling from his Breast the raging God;   ⎬
At length burst out in this prophetick mood: ⎭
    Heavens bless my Son, from *Ireland* let him reign
To farr *Barbadoes* on the Western main;   140
Of his Dominion may no end be known,
And greater than his Father's be his Throne.
Beyond loves Kingdom let him stretch his Pen;
He paus'd, and all the people cry'd *Amen*.
Then thus, continu'd he, my Son advance   145
Still in new Impudence, new Ignorance.
Success let others teach, learn thou from me
Pangs without birth, and fruitless Industry.
Let *Virtuoso's* in five years be Writ;
Yet not one thought accuse thy toyl of wit.   150
Let gentle *George* in triumph tread the Stage,
Make *Dorimant* betray, and *Loveit* rage;
Let *Cully*, *Cockwood*, *Fopling*, charm the Pit,
And in their folly shew the Writers wit.
Yet still thy fools shall stand in thy defence,   155
And justifie their Author's want of sense.
Let 'em be all by thy own model made
Of dullness, and desire no foreign aid:
That they to future ages may be known,
Not Copies drawn, but Issue of thy own.   160
Nay let thy men of wit too be the same,

All full of thee, and differing but in name;
But let no alien *S–dl–y* interpose
To lard with wit thy hungry *Epsom* prose.
And when false flowers of *Rhetorick* thou would'st cull, 165
Trust Nature, do not labour to be dull;
But write thy best, and top; and in each line,
Sir *Formal*'s oratory will be thine.
Sir *Formal*, though unsought, attends thy quill,
And does thy *Northern Dedications* fill. 170
Nor let false friends seduce thy mind to fame,
By arrogating *Johnson*'s Hostile name.
Let Father *Fleckno* fire thy mind with praise,
And Uncle *Ogleby* thy envy raise.
Thou art my blood, where *Johnson* has no part; 175
What share have we in Nature or in Art?
Where did his wit on learning fix a brand,
And rail at Arts he did not understand?
Where made he love in Prince *Nicander*'s vein,
Or swept the dust in *Psyche*'s humble strain? 180
Where sold he Bargains, Whip-stitch, kiss my Arse,
Promis'd a Play and dwindled to a Farce?
When did his Muse from *Fletcher* scenes purloin,
As thou whole *Eth'ridg* dost transfuse to thine?
But so transfus'd as Oyl on Waters flow, 185
His always floats above, thine sinks below.
This is thy Province, this thy wondrous way,
New Humours to invent for each new Play:
This is that boasted Byas of thy mind,
By which one way, to dullness, 'tis inclin'd. 190
Which makes thy writings lean on one side still,
And in all changes that way bends thy will.
Nor let thy mountain belly make pretence
Of likeness; thine's a tympany of sense.

A Tun of Man in thy Large bulk is writ,   195
But sure thou'rt but a Kilderkin of wit.
Like mine thy gentle numbers feebly creep,
Thy Tragick Muse gives smiles, thy Comick sleep.
With whate'er gall thou sett'st thy self to write,
Thy inoffensive Satyrs never bite.   200
In thy fellonious heart, though Venom lies,
It does but touch thy *Irish* pen, and dyes.
Thy Genius calls thee not to purchase fame
In keen Iambicks, but mild Anagram:
Leave writing Plays, and chuse for thy command   205
Some peacefull Province in Acrostick Land.
There thou maist wings display and Altars raise,
And torture one poor word Ten thousand ways.
Or if thou would'st thy diff'rent talents suit,
Set thy own Songs, and sing them to thy lute.   210
He said, but his last words were scarcely heard, ⎫
For *Bruce* and *Longvil* had a *Trap* prepar'd, ⎬
And down they sent the yet declaiming Bard. ⎭
Sinking he left his Drugget robe behind,
Born upwards by a subterranean wind.   215
The Mantle fell to the young Prophet's part,
With double portion of his Father's Art.

From The Second Part of Absalom and Achitophel

Published November 1682

Now stop your noses Readers, all and some, ⎫
For here's a tun of Midnight-work to come, ⎬
Og from a Treason Tavern rowling home. ⎭
Round as a Globe, and Liquor'd ev'ry chink,   [460]

Goodly and Great he Sayls behind his Link;   5
With all this Bulk there's nothing lost in *Og*
For ev'ry inch that is not Fool is Rogue:
A Monstrous mass of foul corrupted matter,
As all the Devils had spew'd to make the batter.
When wine has given him courage to Blaspheme,   10
He Curses God, but God before Curst him;
And if man cou'd have reason none has more,
That made his Paunch so rich and him so poor.
With wealth he was not trusted, for Heav'n knew
What 'twas of Old to pamper up a *Jew*;   15
To what wou'd he on Quail and Pheasant swell,
That ev'n on Tripe and Carrion cou'd rebell?
But though Heav'n made him poor, (with rev'rence speaking,)
He never was a Poet of God's making;
The Midwife laid her hand on his Thick Skull,   20
With this Prophetick blessing—*Be thou Dull;*
Drink, Swear and Roar, forbear no lew'd delight
Fit for thy Bulk, doe any thing but write:
Thou art of lasting Make like thoughtless men,   [480]
A strong Nativity—but for the Pen;   25
Eat Opium, mingle Arsenick in thy Drink,
Still thou mayst live avoiding Pen and Ink.
I see, I see 'tis Counsell given in vain,
For Treason botcht in Rhime will be thy bane;
Rhime is the Rock on which thou art to wreck,   30
'Tis fatal to thy Fame and to thy Neck:
Why shoud thy Metre good King *David* blast?
A Psalm of his will Surely be thy last.
Dar'st thou presume in verse to meet thy foes,
Thou whom the Penny Pamphlet foil'd in prose?   35
Doeg, whom God for Mankinds mirth has made,
O'er-tops thy tallent in thy very Trade;

Doeg to thee, thy paintings are so Course,
A Poet is, though he's the Poets Horse.
A Double Noose thou on thy Neck dost pull,   40
For Writing Treason, and for Writing dull;
To die for Faction is a Common evil,
But to be hang'd for Non-sense is the Devil:
Had'st thou the Glories of thy King exprest,   [500]
Thy praises had been Satyr at the best;   45
But thou in Clumsy verse, unlickt, unpointed,
Hast Shamefully defi'd the Lord's Anointed:
I will not rake the Dunghill of thy Crimes,
For who wou'd reade thy Life that reads thy rhimes?
But of King *David*'s Foes be this the Doom,   50
May all be like the Young-man *Absalom*;
And for my Foes may this their Blessing be,
To talk like *Doeg*, and to Write like Thee.

From Absalom and Achitophel

Published November 1681

WHAT cannot Praise effect in Mighty Minds,
When Flattery Sooths, and when Ambition Blinds!
Desire of Power, on Earth a Vitious Weed,
Yet, sprung from High, is of Cælestial Seed:
In God 'tis Glory: And when men Aspire,   5
'Tis but a Spark too much of Heavenly Fire.
Th' Ambitious Youth, too Covetous of Fame,
Too full of Angells Metal in his Frame;   [310]
Unwarily was led from Vertues ways;
Made Drunk with Honour, and Debauch'd with Praise. 10
Half loath, and half consenting to the Ill,

(For Loyal Blood within him strugled still)
He thus reply'd—And what Pretence have I
To take up Arms for Publick Liberty?
My Father Governs with unquestion'd Right;   15
The Faiths Defender, and Mankinds Delight:
Good, Gracious, Just, observant of the Laws;
And Heav'n by Wonders has Espous'd his Cause.
Whom has he Wrong'd in all his Peaceful Reign?
Who sues for Justice to his Throne in Vain?   20
What Millions has he Pardon'd of his Foes,
Whom Just Revenge did to his Wrath expose?
Mild, Easy, Humble, Studious of our Good;
Enclin'd to Mercy, and averse from Blood.
If Mildness Ill with Stubborn *Israel* Suite,   25
His Crime is God's beloved Attribute.
What could he gain, his People to Betray,
Or change his Right, for Arbitrary Sway?   [330]
Let Haughty *Pharaoh* Curse with such a Reign,
His Fruitfull *Nile*, and Yoak a Servile Train.   30
If *David*'s Rule *Jerusalem* Displease,
The *Dog-star* heats their Brains to this Disease.
Why then shoud I, Encouraging the Bad,
Turn Rebell, and run Popularly Mad?
Were he a Tyrant who, by Lawless Might,   35
Opprest the *Jews*, and Rais'd the *Jebusite*,
Well might I Mourn; but Natures Holy Bands
Woud Curb my Spirits, and Restrain my Hands:
The People might assert their Liberty;
But what was Right in them, were Crime in me.   40
His Favour leaves me nothing to require;
Prevents my Wishes, and outruns Desire.
What more can I expect while *David* lives,
All but his Kingly Diadem he gives;

And that: But there he Paus'd; then Sighing, said,   45
Is justly Destin'd for a Worthier Head.
For when my Father from his Toyls shall Rest,
And late Augment the Number of the Blest: [350]
His Lawfull Issue shall the Throne ascend,
Or the *Collateral* Line where that shall end.   50
His Brother, though Opprest with Vulgar Spight,
Yet Dauntless and Secure of Native Right,
Of every Royal Vertue stands possest;
Still Dear to all the Bravest, and the Best.
His Courage Foes, his Friends his Truth Proclaim;   55
His Loyalty the King, the World his Fame.
His Mercy even th' Offending Crowd will find,
For sure he comes of a Forgiving Kind.
Why shoud I then Repine at Heavens Decree;
Which gives me no Pretence to Royalty?   60
Yet oh that Fate Propitiously Enclind,
Had rais'd my Birth, or had debas'd my Mind;
To my large Soul, not all her Treasure lent,
And then Betray'd it to a mean Descent.
I find, I find my mounting Spirits Bold,   65
And *David*'s Part disdains my Mothers Mold.
Why am I Scanted by a Niggard Birth?
My Soul Disclaims the Kindred of her Earth: [370]
And made for Empire, Whispers me within;
Desire of Greatness is a Godlike Sin.   70
   Him Staggering so when Hells dire Agent found,
While fainting Vertue scarce maintain'd her Ground,
He pours fresh Forces in, and thus Replies:
   Th' Eternal God Supreamly Good and Wise,
Imparts not these Prodigious Gifts in vain;   75
What Wonders are Reserv'd to bless your Reign?
Against your will your Arguments have shown,

Such Vertue's only given to guide a Throne.
Not that your Father's Mildness I contemn;
But Manly Force becomes the Diadem.   80
'Tis true, he grants the People all they crave;
And more perhaps than Subjects ought to have:
For Lavish grants suppose a Monarch tame,
And more his Goodness than his Wit proclaim.
But when shoud People strive their Bonds to break,   85
If not when Kings are Negligent or Weak?
Let him give on till he can give no more,
The Thrifty Sanhedrin shall keep him poor: [390]
And every Sheckle which he can receive,
Shall cost a Limb of his Prerogative.   90
To ply him with new Plots, shall be my care,
Or plunge him deep in some Expensive War;
Which when his Treasure can no more Supply,
He must, with the Remains of Kingship, buy.
His faithful Friends, our Jealousies and Fears,   95
Call *Jebusites*; and *Pharaoh*'s Pentioners:
Whom, when our Fury from his Aid has torn,
He shall be Naked left to publick Scorn.
The next Successor, whom I fear and hate,
My Arts have made Obnoxious to the State;   100
Turn'd all his Vertues to his Overthrow,
And gain'd our Elders to pronounce a Foe.
His Right, for Sums of necessary Gold,
Shall first be Pawn'd, and afterwards be Sold:
Till time shall Ever-wanting *David* draw,   105
To pass your doubtfull Title into Law:
If not; the People have a Right Supreme
To make their Kings; for Kings are made for them.   [410]
All Empire is no more than Pow'r in Trust,
Which when resum'd, can be no longer Just.   110

Succession, for the general Good design'd,
In its own wrong a Nation cannot bind:
If altering that, the People can relieve,
Better one Suffer, than a Nation grieve.
The *Jews* well know their power: e'r *Saul* they Chose,   115
God was their King, and God they durst Depose.
Urge now your Piety, your Filial Name,
A Father's Right, and fear of future Fame;
The publick Good, that Universal Call,
To which even Heav'n Submitted, answers all.   120
Nor let his Love Enchant your generous Mind;
'Tis Natures trick to Propagate her Kind.
Our fond Begetters, who woud never dye,
Love but themselves in their Posterity.
Or let his Kindness by th' Effects be try'd,   125
Or let him lay his vain Pretence aside.
God said he lov'd your Father; coud he bring
A better Proof, than to Anoint him King?   [430]
It surely shew'd he lov'd the Shepherd well,
Who gave so fair a Flock as *Israel*.   130
Woud *David* have you thought his Darling Son?
What means he then, to Alienate the Crown?
The name of Godly he may blush to bear:
'Tis after God's own heart to Cheat his Heir.
He to his Brother gives Supreme Command;   135
To you a Legacy of Barren Land:
Perhaps th' old Harp, on which he thrums his Layes:
Or some dull *Hebrew* Ballad in your Praise.
Then the next Heir, a Prince, Severe and Wise,
Already looks on you with Jealous Eyes;   140
Sees through the thin Disguises of your Arts,
And markes your Progress in the Peoples Hearts.
Though now his mighty Soul its Grief contains;

He meditates Revenge who least Complains.
And like a Lyon, Slumbring in the way,   145
Or Sleep-dissembling, while he waits his Prey,
His fearless Foes within his Distance draws;
Constrains his Roaring, and Contracts his Paws;   [450]
Till at the last, his time for Fury found,
He shoots with suddain Vengeance from the Ground: 150
The Prostrate Vulgar, passes o'r, and Spares;
But with a Lordly Rage, his Hunters teares.
Your Case no tame Expedients will afford;
Resolve on Death, or Conquest by the Sword,
Which for no less a Stake than Life, you Draw;   155
And Self-defence is Natures Eldest Law.
Leave the warm People no Considering time;
For then Rebellion may be thought a Crime.
Prevail your self of what Occasion gives,
But try your Title while your Father lives: 160
And that your Arms may have a fair Pretence,
Proclaim, you take them in the King's Defence:
Whose Sacred Life each minute woud Expose,
To Plots, from seeming Friends, and secret Foes.
And who can sound the depth of *David*'s Soul?   165
Perhaps his fear, his kindness may Controul.
He fears his Brother, though he loves his Son,
For plighted Vows too late to be undone.   [470]
If so, by Force he wishes to be gain'd,
Like womens Leachery, to seem Constrain'd: 170
Doubt not, but when he most affects the Frown,
Commit a pleasing Rape upon the Crown.
Secure his Person to secure your Cause;
They who possess the Prince, possess the Laws.

From Religio Laici

Published November 1682

DIM, as the borrow'd beams of Moon and Stars
To *lonely*, *weary*, *wandring* Travellers,
Is *Reason* to the *Soul*: And as on high,
Those rowling Fires *discover* but the Sky
Not light us *here*; So *Reason*'s glimmering Ray ⎞   5
Was lent, not to *assure* our *doubtfull* way, ⎟
But *guide* us upward to a *better Day*. ⎠
And as those nightly Tapers disappear
When Day's bright Lord ascends our Hemisphere;
So pale grows *Reason* at *Religions* sight;   10
So *dyes*, and so *dissolves* in *Supernatural Light*.
Some few, whose Lamp shone brighter, have been led
From Cause to Cause, to *Natures* secret head;
And found that *one first principle* must be:
But *what*, or *who*, that UNIVERSAL HE;   15
Whether some *Soul* incompassing this Ball
Unmade, *unmov'd*; yet *making*, *moving All*;
Or various *Atoms* interfering Dance
Leapt into *Form*, (the Noble work of *Chance*;)
Or this great *All* was from *Eternity*; ⎞   20
Not ev'n the *Stagirite* himself could see; ⎟
And *Epicurus Guess'd* as well as He: ⎠
As *blindly grop'd* they for a *future State*;
As *rashly Judg'd* of *Providence* and *Fate*:
But least of all could their Endeavours find   25
What most concern'd the good of Humane kind:
For *Happiness* was never to be found;
But vanish'd from 'em, like Enchanted ground.
One thought *Content* the Good to be enjoy'd:

This, every little *Accident* destroy'd: 30
The *wiser Madmen* did for *Vertue* toyl:
A Thorny, or at best a barren Soil:
In *Pleasure* some their glutton Souls would steep; ⎫
But found their Line too short, the Well too deep; ⎬
And leaky Vessels which no *Bliss* cou'd keep.   ⎭ 35
Thus, *anxious Thoughts* in *endless Circles* roul,
Without a *Centre* where to fix the *Soul*:
In this wilde Maze their vain Endeavours end.
How can the *less* the *Greater* comprehend?
Or *finite Reason* reach *Infinity*?   40
For what cou'd *Fathom* GOD were *more* than *He*.

       ★   ★   ★   ★

    Shall I speak plain, and in a Nation free
Assume an honest *Layman's Liberty*?
I think (according to my little Skill,
To my own Mother-Church submitting still:)   45
That many have been sav'd, and many may,   [320]
Who never heard this Question brought in play.
Th' *unletter'd* Christian, who believes in *gross*,
Plods on to *Heaven*; and ne'er is at a loss:
For the *Streight-gate* wou'd be made *streighter* yet,   50
Were *none* admitted there but men of *Wit*.
The few, by Nature form'd, with Learning fraught,
Born to instruct, as others to be taught,
Must Study well the Sacred Page; and see
Which Doctrine, this, or that, does best agree   55
With the whole Tenour of the Work Divine:
And plainlyest points to Heaven's reveal'd Design:
Which Exposition flows from *genuine Sense*;
And which is *forc'd* by *Wit* and *Eloquence*.
Not that Traditions parts are useless here: 60
When general, old, disinteress'd and clear:

That Ancient Fathers thus expound the Page,
Gives *Truth* the reverend Majesty of *Age*:
Confirms its force, by biding every *Test*;
For best *Authority*'s next *Rules* are *best*.   65
And still the nearer to the Spring we go   [340]
More limpid, more unsoyl'd the Waters flow.
Thus, *first Traditions* were a proof alone;
Cou'd we be *certain* such they *were*, so *known*:
But since some Flaws in long descent may be,   70
They make not *Truth* but *Probability*.
Even *Arius* and *Pelagius* durst provoke
To what the *Centuries preceding* spoke.
Such difference is there in an oft-told Tale:
But Truth by its own Sinews will prevail.   75
Tradition written therefore more commends
Authority, than what from *Voice* descends:
And this, as perfect as its kind can be,
Rouls down to us the Sacred History:
Which, from the *Universal Church receiv'd*,   80
Is *try'd*, and *after*, for its *self* believ'd.
    The partial *Papists* wou'd infer from hence
Their Church, in last resort, shou'd Judge the *Sense*.
But first they wou'd assume, with wondrous Art,
Themselves to be the *whole*, who are but *part*   85
Of that vast Frame, the Church; yet grant they were [360]
The handers down, can they from thence infer
A right t' interpret? or wou'd they alone
Who brought the Present, claim it for their own?
The *Book*'s a *Common Largess* to *Mankind*;   90
Not more for *them*, than *every* Man design'd:
The *welcome News* is in the *Letter* found;
The *Carrier*'s not Commission'd to *expound*.
It *speaks* it *Self*, and what it does contain,

In all things *needfull* to be *known*, is *plain*.   95
   In times o'ergrown with Rust and Ignorance,
A gainfull Trade their Clergy did advance:
When want of Learning kept the *Laymen* low,
And none but *Priests* were *Authoriz'd* to *know*:
When what small Knowledge was, in them did dwell; 100
And he a *God* who cou'd but *Reade* or *Spell*;
Then *Mother Church* did mightily prevail:
She parcel'd out the Bible by *retail*:
But still *expounded* what She *sold* or *gave*;
To keep it in *her Power* to *Damn* and *Save*:   105
Scripture was *scarce*, and as the Market went,   [380]
Poor *Laymen* took *Salvation* on *Content*;
As needy men take Money, good or bad:
God's Word they had not, but the *Priests* they had.
Yet, whate'er *false Conveyances* they made,   110
The *Lawyer* still was *certain* to be paid.
In those dark times they learn'd their knack so well,
That by long use they grew *Infallible*:
At last, a knowing Age began t' enquire
If *they* the *Book*, or *That* did *them* inspire: 115
And, making narrower search they found, thô late,
That what they thought the *Priest*'s, was *Their* Estate:
Taught by the *Will produc'd*, (the written Word)
How long they had been *cheated* on *Record*.
Then, every man who saw the Title fair,   120
Claim'd a Child's part, and put in for a Share:
Consulted Soberly his private good;
And sav'd himself as cheap as e'er he cou'd.
   'Tis true, my Friend, (and far be Flattery hence)
This good had full as bad a Consequence: 125
The Book thus put in every vulgar hand,   [400]
Which each presum'd he best cou'd understand,

The *Common Rule* was made the *common Prey*;
And at the mercy of the *Rabble* lay.
The tender Page with horney Fists was gaul'd;   130
And he was gifted most that loudest baul'd:
The *Spirit* gave the *Doctoral Degree*:
And every member of a *Company*
Was of *his Trade*, and of the *Bible free*.
Plain *Truths* enough for needfull *use* they found;   135
But men wou'd still be itching to *expound*:
Each was ambitious of th' obscurest place,
No measure ta'n from *Knowledge*, all from *GRACE*.
Study and *Pains* were now no more their Care;
Texts were explain'd by *Fasting*, and by *Prayer*:   140
This was the Fruit the *private Spirit* brought;
Occasion'd by *great Zeal*, and *little Thought*.
While Crouds unlearn'd, with rude Devotion warm,
About the Sacred Viands buz and swarm,
The *Fly-blown Text* creates a *crawling Brood*;   145
And turns to *Maggots* what was meant for *Food*.   [420]
A Thousand daily Sects rise up, and dye;
A Thousand more the perish'd Race supply.
So all we make of Heavens discover'd Will
Is, not to have it, or to use it ill.   150
The Danger's much the same; on several Shelves
If *others* wreck *us*, or *we* wreck our *selves*.
   What then remains, but, waving each Extreme,
The Tides of Ignorance, and Pride to stem?
Neither so rich a Treasure to forgo;   155
Nor proudly seek beyond our pow'r to know:
Faith is not built on disquisitions vain;
The things we *must* believe, are *few*, and *plain*:
But since men *will* believe more than they *need*;
And every man will make *himself* a Creed: 160

In doubtfull questions 'tis the safest way
To learn what unsuspected Ancients say:
For 'tis not likely *we* shou'd higher Soar
In search of Heav'n, than *all the Church before*:
Nor can we be deceiv'd, unless we see   165
The *Scripture*, and the *Fathers disagree*.   [440]
If after all, they stand suspected still,
(For no man's Faith depends upon his Will;)
'Tis some Relief, that points not clearly known,
Without much hazard may be let alone: 170
And, after hearing what our Church can say,
If still our Reason runs another way,
That private Reason 'tis more Just to curb,
Than by Disputes the publick Peace disturb.
For points obscure are of small use to learn: 175
But *Common quiet* is *Mankind's concern*.
    Thus have I made my own Opinions clear:
Yet neither Praise expect, nor Censure fear:
And this unpolish'd, rugged Verse, I chose;
As fittest for Discourse, and nearest Prose: 180
For, while from *Sacred Truth* I do not swerve,
Tom Sternhold's, or *Tom Shadwell*'s *Rhimes* will serve.

From The Hind and the Panther

Written in winter 1686–7. Published May 1687

WHAT weight of antient witness can prevail
If private reason hold the publick scale?
But, gratious God, how well dost thou provide
For erring judgments an unerring Guide?
Thy throne is darkness in th' abyss of light,   5

A blaze of glory that forbids the sight;
O teach me to believe Thee thus conceal'd,
And search no farther than thy self reveal'd;
But her alone for my Directour take   [70]
Whom thou hast promis'd never to forsake!   10
My thoughtless youth was wing'd with vain desires,
My manhood, long misled by wandring fires,
Follow'd false lights; and when their glimps was gone,
My pride struck out new sparkles of her own.
Such was I, such by nature still I am,   15
Be thine the glory, and be mine the shame.
Good life be now my task: my doubts are done,
(What more could fright my faith, than Three in One?)
Can I believe eternal God could lye   ⎫
Disguis'd in mortal mold and infancy?   ⎬   20
That the great maker of the world could dye? ⎭
And after that, trust my imperfect sense
Which calls in question his omnipotence?
Can I my reason to my faith compell,
And shall my sight, and touch, and taste rebell?   25
Superiour faculties are set aside,
Shall their subservient organs be my guide?
Then let the moon usurp the rule of day,
And winking tapers shew the sun his way;   [90]
For what my senses can themselves perceive   30
I need no revelation to believe.
Can they who say the Host should be descry'd
By sense, define a body glorify'd?
Impassible, and penetrating parts?
Let them declare by what mysterious arts   35
He shot that body through th' opposing might ⎫
Of bolts and barrs impervious to the light, ⎬
And stood before his train confess'd in open sight. ⎭

    For since thus wondrously he pass'd, 'tis plain
One single place two bodies did contain,   40
And sure the same omnipotence as well
Can make one body in more places dwell.
Let reason then at Her own quarry fly,
But how can finite grasp infinity?
    'Tis urg'd again that faith did first commence   45
By miracles, which are appeals to sense,
And thence concluded that our sense must be
The motive still of credibility.
For latter ages must on former wait,   [110]
And what began belief, must propagate.   50
    But winnow well this thought, and you shall find,
'Tis light as chaff that flies before the wind.
Were all those wonders wrought by pow'r divine
As means or ends of some more deep design?
Most sure as means, whose end was this alone,   55
To prove the god-head of th' eternal Son.
God thus asserted: man is to believe
Beyond what sense and reason can conceive.
And for mysterious things of faith rely
On the Proponent, heav'ns authority.   60
If then our faith we for our guide admit,
Vain is the farther search of humane wit,
As when the building gains a surer stay,
We take th' unusefull scaffolding away:
Reason by sense no more can understand,   65
The game is play'd into another hand.
Why chuse we then like *Bilanders* to creep ⎫
Along the coast, and land in view to keep, ⎬
When safely we may launch into the deep? ⎭   [130]
In the same vessel which our Saviour bore   70
Himself the Pilot, let us leave the shoar,

And with a better guide a better world explore.
Could He his god-head veil with flesh and bloud
And not veil these again to be our food?
His grace in both is equal in extent,   75
The first affords us life, the second nourishment.
And if he can, why all this frantick pain
To construe what his clearest words contain,⎫
And make a riddle what He made so plain?   ⎬
To take up half on trust, and half to try,   ⎭   80
Name it not faith, but bungling biggottry.
Both knave and fool the Merchant we may call   ⎫
To pay great summs, and to compound the small.   ⎬
For who wou'd break with heav'n, and wou'd not break for all?⎭
Rest then, my soul, from endless anguish freed;   85
Nor sciences thy guide, nor sense thy creed.
Faith is the best ensurer of thy bliss;
The Bank above must fail before the venture miss.

★   ★   ★   ★

FROM THE SECOND PART

Now, to remove the least remaining doubt,
That ev'n the blear-ey'd sects may find her out,   90
Behold what heav'nly rays adorn her brows,   ⎫
What from his Wardrobe her belov'd allows   ⎬
To deck the wedding-day of his unspotted spouse.⎭
Behold what marks of majesty she brings;   [520]
Richer than ancient heirs of Eastern kings: 95
Her right hand holds the sceptre and the keys,
To shew whom she commands, and who obeys:
With these to bind, or set the sinner free,
With that t' assert spiritual Royalty.
    One in herself not rent by schism, but sound,   100
Entire, one solid shining Diamond,

Not sparkles shatter'd into sects like you,
One is the church, and must be to be true:
One central principle of unity.
As undivided, so from errours free,   105
As one in faith, so one in sanctity.
Thus she, and none but she, th' insulting rage
Of Hereticks oppos'd from age to age:
Still when the Gyant-brood invades her throne
She stoops from heav'n, and meets 'em half way down,   110
And with paternal thunder vindicates her crown.
But like *Ægyptian* Sorcerers you stand,
And vainly lift aloft your magick wand,
To sweep away the swarms of vermin from the land: [540]
You cou'd like them, with like infernal force   115
Produce the plague, but not arrest the course.
But when the boils and botches, with disgrace
And publick scandal sat upon the face,
Themselves attack'd, the *Magi* strove no more,
They saw God's finger, and their fate deplore;   120
Themselves they cou'd not cure of the dishonest sore.
    Thus one, thus pure, behold her largely spread
Like the fair ocean from her mother bed;
From East to West triumphantly she rides,
All shoars are water'd by her wealthy Tides.   125
    The Gospel-sound diffus'd from Pole to Pole,
Where winds can carry, and where waves can roll.
The self same doctrine of the Sacred page
Convey'd to ev'ry clime in ev'ry age.

★   ★   ★   ★

FROM THE THIRD PART

A Portly Prince, and goodly to the sight,   130
He seem'd a Son of *Anach* for his height:

Like those whom stature did to Crowns prefer;
Black-brow'd, and bluff, like *Homer*'s *Jupiter*:
Broad-back'd, and Brawny built for Loves delight,
A Prophet form'd, to make a female Proselyte.   135
A Theologue more by need than genial bent,
By Breeding sharp, by Nature confident.
Int'rest in all his Actions was discern'd;
More learn'd than Honest, more a Wit than learn'd.   [1150]
Or forc'd by Fear, or by his Profit led,   140
Or both conjoyn'd, his Native clime he fled:
But brought the Vertues of his Heav'n along;
A fair Behaviour, and a fluent Tongue.
And yet with all his Arts he could not thrive;
The most unlucky Parasite alive.   145
Loud Praises to prepare his Paths he sent,
And then himself pursu'd his Compliment:
But, by reverse of Fortune chac'd away,
His Gifts no longer than their Author stay:
He shakes the Dust against th' ungrateful race,   150
And leaves the stench of Ordures in the place.
Oft has he flatter'd, and blasphem'd the same,
For in his Rage, he spares no Sov'rains name:
The Hero, and the Tyrant change their style
By the same measure that they frown or smile;   155
When well receiv'd by hospitable Foes,
The kindness he returns, is to expose:
For Courtesies, tho' undeserv'd and great, ⎱
No gratitude in Fellon-minds beget,   ⎰   [1170]
As tribute to his Wit, the churl receives the treat. ⎰   160
His praise of Foes is venemously Nice, ⎱
So touch'd, it turns a Vertue to a Vice: ⎰
A Greek, *and bountiful forewarns us twice.* ⎰
Sev'n Sacraments he wisely do's disown,

Because he knows Confession stands for one;   165
Where Sins to sacred silence are convey'd,
And not for Fear, or Love, to be betray'd:
But he, uncall'd, his Patron to controul,
Divulg'd the secret whispers of his Soul:
Stood forth th' accusing *Sathan* of his Crimes,   170
And offer'd to the *Moloch* of the Times.
Prompt to assayle, and careless of defence,
Invulnerable in his Impudence;
He dares the World, and eager of a name,
He thrusts about, and justles into fame.   175
Frontless, and Satyr-proof he scow'rs the streets,
And runs an *Indian* muck at all he meets.
So fond of loud Report, that not to miss
Of being known (his last and utmost bliss)   [1190]
He rather would be known, for what he is.   180

From The Third Satyr of Juvenal

Published early in 1693

RETURN we to the Dangers of the Night;
And, first, behold our Houses dreadful height: [430]
From whence come broken Potsherds tumbling down;
And leaky Ware, from Garret Windows thrown:
Well may they break our Heads, that mark the flinty Stone. 5
'Tis want of Sence to sup abroad too late;
Unless thou first hast settled thy Estate.
As many Fates attend, thy Steps to meet,
As there are waking Windows in the Street.
Bless the good Gods, and think thy chance is rare   10
To have a Piss-pot only for thy share.

The scouring Drunkard, if he does not fight
Before his Bed-time, takes no rest that Night.
Passing the tedious Hours in greater pain
Than stern *Achilles*, when his Friend was slain: 15
'Tis so ridic'lous, but so true withall,
A Bully cannot sleep without a Braul.
Yet tho his youthful Blood be fir'd with Wine,
He wants not Wit, the Danger to decline:
Is cautious to avoid the Coach and Six,   20
And on the Lacquies will no Quarrel fix.
His Train of Flambeaus, and Embroider'd Coat   [450]
May Priviledge my Lord to walk secure on Foot.
But me, who must by Moon-light homeward bend,
Or lighted only with a Candle's end,   25
Poor me he fights, if that be fighting, where
He only Cudgels, and I only bear.
He stands, and bids me stand: I must abide;
For he's the stronger, and is Drunk beside.

Where did you whet your Knife to Night, he cries,   30
And shred the Leeks that in your Stomach rise?
Whose windy Beans have stuff't your Guts, and where
Have your black Thumbs been dipt in Vinegar?
With what Companion Cobler have you fed,
On old Ox-cheeks, or He-Goats tougher Head?   35
What, are you Dumb? Quick with your Answer, quick;
Before my Foot Salutes you with a Kick.
Say, in what nasty Cellar, under Ground,
Or what Church-Porch your Rogueship may be found?
Answer, or Answer not, 'tis all the same: 40
He lays me on, and makes me bear the blame.
Before the Bar, for beating him, you come;   [470]
This is a Poor Man's Liberty in *Rome*.
You beg his Pardon; happy to retreat

With some remaining Teeth, to chew your Meat.   45
  Nor is this all: for, when Retir'd, you think
To sleep securely; when the Candles wink,
When every Door with Iron Chains is barr'd,
And roaring Taverns are no longer heard;
The Ruffian Robbers, by no Justice aw'd,   50
And unpaid cut-Throat Soldiers are abroad.
Those Venal Souls, who harden'd in each ill
To save Complaints and Prosecution, kill.
Chas'd from their Woods and Bogs the Padders come ⎫
To this vast City, as their Native Home: ⎬   55
To live at ease, and safely sculk in *Rome*.   ⎭
  The Forge in Fetters only is employ'd;
Our Iron Mines exhausted and destroy'd
In Shackles; for these Villains scarce allow
Goads for the Teams, and Plough-shares for the Plough.   60
Oh happy Ages of our Ancestours,
Beneath the Kings and Tribunitial Pow'rs!   [490]
One Jayl did all their Criminals restrain;
Which, now, the Walls of *Rome* can scarce contain.
  More I cou'd say; more Causes I cou'd show   65
For my departure; but the Sun is low:
The Waggoner grows weary of my stay;
And whips his Horses forwards on their way.
  Farewell; and when, like me, o'rewhelm'd with care, ⎫
You to your own *Aquinum* shall repair,   ⎬   70
To take a mouthful of sweet Country air,   ⎭
Be mindful of your Friend; and send me word,
What Joys your Fountains and cool Shades afford:
Then, to assist your Satyrs, I will come:
And add new Venom, when you write of *Rome*.   75

From Lucretius. The beginning of the Second Book

Published early in 1685

'Tis pleasant, safely to behold from shore
The rowling Ship; and hear the Tempest roar:
Not that anothers pain is our delight;
But pains unfelt produce the pleasing sight.
'Tis pleasant also to behold from far   5
The moving Legions mingled in the War:
But much more sweet thy lab'ring steps to guide,
To Vertues heights, with wisdom well supply'd,
And all the *Magazins* of Learning fortifi'd:
From thence to look below on humane kind,   10
Bewilder'd in the Maze of Life, and blind:
To see vain fools ambitiously contend
For Wit and Pow'r; their lost endeavours bend
T'outshine each other, waste their time and health,
In search of honour, and pursuit of wealth.   15
O wretched man! in what a mist of Life,
Inclos'd with dangers and with noisie strife,
He spends his little Span: And overfeeds
His cramm'd desires, with more than nature needs:
For Nature wisely stints our appetite,   20
And craves no more than undisturb'd delight;
Which minds unmix'd with cares, and fears, obtain;
A Soul serene, a body void of pain.
So little this corporeal frame requires;
So bounded are our natural desires,   25
That wanting all, and setting pain aside,
With bare privation, sence is satisfi'd.

If Golden Sconces hang not on the Walls,
To light the costly Suppers and the Balls;
If the proud Palace shines not with the state   30
Of burnish'd Bowls, and of reflected Plate,
If well tun'd Harps, nor the more pleasing sound
Of Voices, from the vaulted roofs rebound,
Yet on the grass beneath a poplar shade
By the cool stream, our careless limbs are lay'd,   35
With cheaper pleasures innocently blest,
When the warm Spring with gawdy flow'rs is drest.
Nor will the rageing Feavours fire abate,
With Golden Canopies and Beds of State:
But the poor Patient will as soon be sound,   40
On the hard mattress, or the Mother ground.
Then since our Bodies are not eas'd the more
By Birth, or Pow'r, or Fortunes wealthy store,
Tis plain, these useless toyes of every kind
As little can relieve the lab'ring mind: 45
Unless we cou'd suppose the dreadful sight
Of marshall'd Legions moving to the fight
Cou'd with their sound, and terrible array
Expel our fears, and drive the thoughts of death away.
But since the supposition vain appears,   50
Since clinging cares, and trains of inbred fears,
Are not with sounds to be affrighted thence,
But in the midst of Pomp pursue the Prince,
Not aw'd by arms, but in the presence bold,
Without respect to Purple, or to Gold;   55
Why shou'd not we these pageantries despise;
Whose worth but in our want of reason lies?
For life is all in wandring errours led;
And just as Children are surpriz'd with dread,
And tremble in the dark, so riper years   60

Ev'n in broad day light are possest with fears:
And shake at shadows fanciful and vain,
As those which in the breasts of Children reign.
These bugbears of the mind, this inward Hell,
No rayes of outward sunshine can dispel;   65
But nature and right reason, must display
Their beames abroad, and bring the darksome soul to day.

To the Memory of Mr. Oldham

Written 1683. Published 1684

FAREWEL, too little and too lately known,
Whom I began to think and call my own;
For sure our Souls were near ally'd; and thine
Cast in the same Poetick mould with mine.
One common Note on either Lyre did strike,   5
And Knaves and Fools we both abhorr'd alike:
To the same Goal did both our Studies drive,
The last set out the soonest did arrive.
Thus *Nisus* fell upon the slippery place,
While his young Friend perform'd and won the Race.   10
O early ripe! to thy abundant store
What could advancing Age have added more?
It might (what Nature never gives the young)
Have taught the numbers of thy native Tongue.
But Satyr needs not those, and Wit will shine   15
Through the harsh cadence of a rugged line.
A noble Error, and but seldom made,
When Poets are by too much force betray'd.
Thy generous fruits, though gather'd ere their prime ⎫
Still shew'd a quickness; and maturing time   ⎬ 20
But mellows what we write to the dull sweets of Rime. ⎭

Once more, hail and farewel; farewel thou young,
But ah too short, *Marcellus* of our Tongue;
Thy Brows with Ivy, and with Laurels bound;
But Fate and gloomy Night encompass thee around.   25

Song from Tyrannick Love

Performed June 1669. Published 1670

A H how sweet it is to love,
Ah how gay is young desire!
And what pleasing pains we prove
When we first approach Loves fire!
  Pains of Love be sweeter far   5
  Than all other pleasures are.

Sighs which are from Lovers blown,
Do but gently heave the Heart:
Ev'n the tears they shed alone
Cure, like trickling Balm their smart.   10
  Lovers when they lose their breath,
  Bleed away in easie death.

Love and Time with reverence use,
Treat 'em like a parting friend:
Nor the golden gifts refuse   15
Which in youth sincere they send:
  For each year their price is more,
  And they less simple than before.

Love, like Spring-tides full and high,
Swells in every youthful vein: 20

But each Tide does less supply,
Till they quite shrink in again:
  If a flow in Age appear,
  'Tis but rain, and runs not clear.

Venus's Song from King Arthur

Performed and published May/June 1691

FAIREST Isle, all Isles Excelling,
  Seat of Pleasures, and of Loves;
Venus here, will chuse her Dwelling,
  And forsake her *Cyprian* Groves.

2

Cupid, from his Fav'rite Nation,   5
  Care and Envy will Remove;
Jealousie, that poysons Passion,
  And Despair that dies for Love.

3

Gentle Murmurs, sweet Complaining,
  Sighs that blow the Fire of Love;   10
Soft Repulses, kind Disdaining,
  Shall be all the Pains you prove.

4

Every Swain shall pay his Duty,
  Grateful every Nymph shall prove;
And as these Excel in Beauty,   15
  Those shall be Renown'd for Love.

Song to a Fair, Young Lady, Going out of the Town in the Spring

Examen Poeticum (1693)

1

ASK not the Cause, why sullen *Spring*
   So long delays her Flow'rs to bear;
Why warbling Birds forget to sing,
   And Winter Storms invert the Year?
Chloris is gone; and Fate provides   5
To make it *Spring*, where she resides.

2

Chloris is gone, the Cruel Fair;
   She cast not back a pitying Eye:
But left her Lover in Despair;
   To sigh, to languish, and to die: 10
Ah, how can those fair Eyes endure
To give the Wounds they will not cure!

3

Great God of Love, why hast thou made
   A Face that can all Hearts command,
That all Religions can invade,   15
   And change the Laws of ev'ry Land?
Where thou hadst plac'd such Pow'r before,
Thou shou'dst have made her Mercy more.

4

When *Chloris* to the Temple comes,
   Adoring Crowds before her fall;   20
She can restore the Dead from Tombs,
   And ev'ry Life but mine recall.
I only am by Love design'd
To be the Victim for Mankind.

A Song for St. Cecilia's Day, 1687

I

FROM Harmony, from heav'nly Harmony
   This universal Frame began.
  When Nature underneath a heap
   Of jarring Atomes lay,
  And cou'd not heave her Head,   5
The tuneful Voice was heard from high,
   Arise ye more than dead.
Then cold, and hot, and moist, and dry,
In order to their stations leap,
   And MUSICK's pow'r obey.   10
From Harmony, from heav'nly Harmony
   This universal Frame began:
   From Harmony to Harmony
Through all the compass of the Notes it ran,
The Diapason closing full in Man.   15

II

What Passion cannot MUSICK raise and quell!
   When *Jubal* struck the corded Shell,
  His list'ning Brethren stood around
   And wond'ring, on their Faces fell
  To worship that Celestial Sound.   20
Less than a God they thought there cou'd not dwell
   Within the hollow of that Shell
   That spoke so sweetly and so well.
What Passion cannot MUSICK raise and quell!

III

    The TRUMPETS loud Clangor   25
     Excites us to Arms
    With shrill Notes of Anger
     And mortal Alarms.

The double double double beat
  Of the thundring DRUM   30
    Cryes, hark the Foes come;
  Charge, Charge, 'tis too late to retreat.

IV

The soft complaining FLUTE
In dying Notes discovers
The Woes of hopeless Lovers,   35
Whose Dirge is whisper'd by the warbling LUTE.

V

Sharp VIOLINS proclaim
Their jealous Pangs, and Desperation,
Fury, frantick Indignation,
Depth of Pains, and height of Passion,   40
  For the fair, disdainful Dame.

VI

But oh! what Art can teach
  What human Voice can reach
The sacred ORGANS praise?
Notes inspiring holy Love,   45
Notes that wing their heav'nly ways
  To mend the Choires above.

VII

Orpheus cou'd lead the savage race;
And Trees unrooted left their place;
  Sequacious of the Lyre: 50
But bright *CECILIA* rais'd the wonder high'r;
When to her ORGAN, vocal Breath was giv'n
An Angel heard, and straight appear'd
  Mistaking Earth for Heaven.

Grand CHORUS

As from the pow'r of sacred Lays   55
     The Spheres began to move,
And sung the great Creator's praise
     To all the bless'd above;
So when the last and dreadful hour
This crumbling Pageant shall devour,   60
The TRUMPET *shall be heard on high,*
The Dead shall live, the Living die,
And MUSICK *shall untune the Sky.*

Alexander's Feast; or The Power of Musique. An Ode, in Honour of St. Cecilia's Day

(1697)

I

'TWAS at the Royal Feast, for *Persia* won,
     By *Philip*'s Warlike Son:
   Aloft in awful State
   The God-like Heroe sate
     On his Imperial Throne: 5
  His valiant Peers were plac'd around;
Their Brows with Roses and with Myrtles bound.
  (So shou'd Desert in Arms be Crown'd:)
The Lovely *Thais* by his side,
Sate like a blooming *Eastern* Bride   10
In Flow'r of Youth and Beauty's Pride.
   Happy, happy, happy Pair!
   None but the Brave
   None but the Brave
   None but the Brave deserves the Fair.   15

CHORUS
Happy, happy, happy Pair!
None but the Brave
None but the Brave
None but the Brave deserves the Fair.

II

Timotheus plac'd on high   20
  Amid the tuneful Quire,
   With flying Fingers touch'd the Lyre:
The trembling Notes ascend the Sky,
                      And Heav'nly Joys inspire.

The Song began from *Jove*;   25
Who left his blissful Seats above,
(Such is the Pow'r of mighty Love.)
A Dragon's fiery Form bely'd the God:
Sublime on Radiant Spires He rode,
   When He to fair *Olympia* press'd: 30
   And while He sought her snowy Breast:
Then, round her slender Waste he curl'd,
And stamp'd an Image of himself, a Sov'raign of the World.
The list'ning Crowd admire the lofty Sound,
A present Deity, they shout around: 35
A present Deity the vaulted Roofs rebound.
       With ravish'd Ears
       The Monarch hears,
       Assumes the God,
       Affects to nod,   40
And seems to shake the Spheres.

CHORUS
With ravish'd Ears
The Monarch hears,

Assumes the God,
Affects to Nod,   45
And seems to shake the Spheres.

III

The Praise of *Bacchus* then, the sweet Musician sung;
  Of *Bacchus* ever Fair, and ever Young:
    The jolly God in Triumph comes;
      Sound the Trumpets; beat the Drums: 50
        Flush'd with a purple Grace
        He shews his honest Face,
Now give the Hautboys breath; He comes, He comes.
      Bacchus ever Fair and Young,
        Drinking Joys did first ordain: 55
      Bacchus Blessings are a Treasure;
      Drinking is the Soldiers Pleasure;
        Rich the Treasure,
        Sweet the Pleasure;
      Sweet is Pleasure after Pain.   60

CHORUS

Bacchus Blessings are a Treasure;
Drinking is the Soldier's Pleasure:
Rich the Treasure,
Sweet the Pleasure;
Sweet is Pleasure after Pain.   65

IV

Sooth'd with the Sound the King grew vain;
  Fought all his Battails o'er again;
And thrice He routed all his Foes; and thrice He slew the slain.
    The Master saw the Madness rise;
    His glowing Cheeks, his ardent Eyes;   70

And while He Heav'n and Earth defy'd,
Chang'd his hand, and check'd his Pride.
    He chose a Mournful Muse
    Soft Pity to infuse:
He sung *Darius* Great and Good,   75
    By too severe a Fate,
Fallen, fallen, fallen, fallen,
    Fallen from his high Estate
        And weltring in his Blood:
Deserted at his utmost Need,   80
By those his former Bounty fed:
On the bare Earth expos'd He lyes,
With not a Friend to close his Eyes.

With down-cast Looks the joyless Victor sate,
    Revolveing in his alter'd Soul   85
    The various Turns of Chance below;
And, now and then, a Sigh he stole;
    And Tears began to flow.

CHORUS
Revolveing in his alter'd Soul
    The various Turns of Chance below;
And, now and then, a Sigh he stole;   90
And Tears began to flow.

V
The Mighty Master smil'd to see
That Love was in the next Degree:
'Twas but a Kindred-Sound to move;   95
For Pity melts the Mind to Love.
    Softly sweet, in *Lydian* Measures,
    Soon He sooth'd his Soul to Pleasures.
    War, he sung, is Toil and Trouble;
    Honour but an empty Bubble.   100

Never ending, still beginning,
Fighting still, and still destroying,
If the World be worth thy Winning,
Think, O think, it worth Enjoying.
Lovely *Thais* sits beside thee,   105
Take the Good the Gods provide thee.

The Many rend the Skies, with loud Applause;
So Love was Crown'd, but Musique won the Cause.
The Prince, unable to conceal his Pain,
Gaz'd on the Fair   110
Who caus'd his Care,
And sigh'd and look'd, sigh'd and look'd,
Sigh'd and look'd, and sigh'd again:
At length, with Love and Wine at once oppress'd,
The vanquish'd Victor sunk upon her Breast.   115

CHORUS

The Prince, unable to conceal his Pain,
Gaz'd on the Fair
Who caus'd his Care,
And sigh'd and look'd, sigh'd and look'd,
Sigh'd and look'd, and sigh'd again: 120
At length, with Love and Wine at once oppress'd,
The vanquish'd Victor sunk upon her Breast.

VI

Now strike the Golden Lyre again:
A lowder yet, and yet a lowder Strain.
Break his Bands of Sleep asunder,   125
And rouze him, like a rattling Peal of Thunder.
Hark, hark, the horrid Sound
Has rais'd up his Head,
As awak'd from the Dead,
And amaz'd, he stares around.   130

Revenge, Revenge, *Timotheus* cries,
  See the Furies arise!
  See the Snakes that they rear,
  How they hiss in their Hair,
 And the Sparkles that flash from their Eyes! 135
  Behold a ghastly Band,
  Each a Torch in his Hand!
Those are *Grecian* Ghosts, that in Battail were slayn,
    And unbury'd remain
    Inglorious on the Plain. 140
   Give the Vengeance due
   To the Valiant Crew.
Behold how they toss their Torches on high,
  How they point to the *Persian* Abodes,
And glitt'ring Temples of their Hostile Gods! 145
The Princes applaud, with a furious Joy;
And the King seyz'd a Flambeau, with Zeal to destroy;
   Thais led the Way,
   To light him to his Prey,
And, like another *Hellen*, fir'd another *Troy*. 150

CHORUS
And the King seyz'd a Flambeau, with Zeal to destroy;
   Thais *led the Way,*
   To light him to his Prey,
And, like another Hellen, *fir'd another* Troy.

VII
  Thus, long ago 155
'Ere heaving Bellows learn'd to blow,
  While Organs yet were mute;
Timotheus, to his breathing Flute,
  And sounding Lyre,
Cou'd swell the Soul to rage, or kindle soft Desire. 160

At last Divine *Cecilia* came,
Inventress of the Vocal Frame;
The sweet Enthusiast, from her Sacred Store,
  Enlarg'd the former narrow Bounds,
  And added Length to solemn Sounds,   165
With Nature's Mother-Wit, and Arts unknown before.
  Let old *Timotheus* yield the Prize,
   Or both divide the Crown;
  He rais'd a Mortal to the Skies;
   She drew an Angel down.   170

Grand CHORUS

At last Divine Cecilia *came,*
Inventress of the Vocal Frame;
The sweet Enthusiast, from her Sacred Store,
  Enlarg'd the former narrow Bounds,
  And added Length to solemn Sounds, 175
With Nature's Mother-Wit, and Arts unknown before.
  Let old Timotheus *yield the Prize,*
   Or both divide the Crown;
  He rais'd a Mortal to the Skies;
   She drew an Angel down.   180

The Secular Masque from The Pilgrim

Written before April 1700. Published 1700

Enter JANUS

Janus. CHRONOS, *Chronos*, mend thy Pace,
    An hundred times the rowling Sun
    Around the Radiant Belt has run
    In his revolving Race.
    Behold, behold, the Goal in sight,   5
    Spread thy Fans, and wing thy flight.

Enter CHRONOS, *with a Scythe in his hand, and a great Globe on his*
Back, which he sets down at his entrance

Chronos.   Weary, weary of my weight,
     Let me, let me drop my Freight,
      And leave the World behind.
     I could not bear   10
     Another Year
     The Load of Human-Kind.

     Enter MOMUS *Laughing*

Momus.   Ha! ha! ha! Ha! ha! ha! well hast thou done,
     To lay down thy Pack,
     And lighten thy Back,   15
     The World was a Fool, e'er since it begun,
     And since neither *Janus*, nor *Chronos*, nor I,
     Can hinder the Crimes,
     Or mend the Bad Times,
     'Tis better to Laugh than to Cry. 20
Cho. of all 3. *'Tis better to Laugh than to Cry.*
Janus.   Since *Momus* comes to laugh below,
     Old Time begin the Show,
     That he may see, in every Scene,
     What Changes in this Age have been, 25
Chronos.   Then Goddess of the Silver Bow begin.

     Horns, or Hunting-Musique within
      Enter DIANA

Diana.   With Horns and with Hounds I waken the Day,
     And hye to my Woodland walks away;
     I tuck up my Robe, and am buskin'd soon,
     And tye to my Forehead a wexing Moon. 30
     I course the fleet Stagg, unkennel the Fox,
     And chase the wild Goats or'e summets of
     Rocks,

	With shouting and hooting we pierce thro' the Sky;
	And Eccho turns Hunter, and doubles the Cry.
Cho. of all.	*With shouting and hooting, we pierce through the Skie,* 35
	And Eccho turns Hunter, and doubles the Cry.
Janus.	Then our Age was in it's Prime,
Chronos.	Free from Rage.
Diana.	————————And free from Crime.
Momus.	A very Merry, Dancing, Drinking, 40
	Laughing, Quaffing, and unthinking Time.
Cho. of all.	*Then our Age was in it's Prime,*
	Free from Rage, and free from Crime,
	A very Merry, Dancing, Drinking,
	Laughing, Quaffing, and unthinking Time. 45

Dance of DIANA's *Attendants*

Enter MARS

Mars.	Inspire the Vocal Brass, Inspire;
	The World is past its Infant Age:
	Arms and Honour,
	Arms and Honour,
	Set the Martial Mind on Fire, 50
	And kindle Manly Rage.
	Mars has lookt the Sky to Red;
	And Peace, the Lazy Good, is fled.
	Plenty, Peace, and Pleasure fly;
	The Sprightly Green 55
	In *Woodland*-Walks, no more is seen;
	The Sprightly Green, has drunk the *Tyrian* Dye.
Cho. of all.	*Plenty, Peace, &c.*
Mars.	Sound the Trumpet, Beat the Drum,
	Through all the World around;

	Sound a Reveille, Sound, Sound,	60
	The Warrior God is come.	
Cho. of all.	*Sound the Trumpet*, &c.	
Momus.	Thy Sword within the Scabbard keep,	
	And let Mankind agree;	
	Better the World were fast asleep,	
	Than kept awake by Thee.	65
	The Fools are only thinner,	
	With all our Cost and Care;	
	But neither side a winner,	
	For Things are as they were.	
Cho. of all.	*The Fools are only*, &c.	

Enter VENUS

	Calms appear, when Storms are past;	70
Venus.	Love will have his Hour at last:	
	Nature is my kindly Care;	
	Mars destroys, and I repair;	
	Take me, take me, while you may,	
	Venus comes not ev'ry Day.	75
Cho. of all.	*Take her, take her*, &c.	
Chronos.	The World was then so light,	
	I scarcely felt the Weight;	
	Joy rul'd the Day, and Love the Night.	
	But since the Queen of Pleasure left the Ground,	
	I faint, I lag,	80
	And feebly drag	
	The pond'rous Orb around.	
Momus.	All, all, of a piece throughout;	
Pointing } to *Diana.*	Thy Chase had a Beast in View;	
to *Mars.*	Thy Wars brought nothing about;	85
to *Venus.*	Thy Lovers were all untrue.	

Janus.	'Tis well an Old Age is out,
Chro[nos].	And time to begin a New.
Cho. of all.	*All, all, of a piece throughout;*
	Thy Chase had a Beast in View; 90
	Thy Wars brought nothing about;
	Thy Lovers were all untrue.
	'Tis well an Old Age is out,
	And time to begin a New.

Dance of Huntsmen, Nymphs, Warriours and Lovers.

Horace Lib. I. Ode 9

Sylvae (1685)

I

BEHOLD yon' Mountains hoary height
   Made higher with new Mounts of Snow;
Again behold the Winters weight
   Oppress the lab'ring Woods below:
And streams with Icy fetters bound,   5
Benum'd and crampt to solid ground.

II

With well heap'd Logs dissolve the cold,
   And feed the genial hearth with fires;
Produce the Wine, that makes us bold,
   And sprightly Wit and Love inspires: 10
For what hereafter shall betide,
God, if 'tis worth his care, provide.

III

Let him alone with what he made,
   To toss and turn the World below;
At his command the storms invade;   15
   The winds by his Commission blow:

Till with a Nod he bids 'em cease,
And then the Calm returns, and all is peace.

IV

To morrow and her works defie,
   Lay hold upon the present hour,   20
And snatch the pleasures passing by,
   To put them out of Fortunes pow'r:
Nor love, nor love's delights disdain,
What e're thou get'st to day is gain.

V

Secure those golden early joyes,   25
   That Youth unsowr'd with sorrow bears,
E're with'ring time the taste destroyes,
   With sickness and unweildy years!
For active sports, for pleasing rest,
This is the time to be possest;   30
The best is but in season best.

VI

The pointed hour of promis'd bliss,
   The pleasing whisper in the dark,
The half unwilling willing kiss,
   The laugh that guides thee to the mark,   35
When the kind Nymph wou'd coyness feign,
And hides but to be found again,
These, these are joyes the Gods for Youth ordain.

From Annus Mirabilis. The Year of Wonders, 1666. An Historical Poem

Published early in 1667

SWELL'D with our late successes on the Foe,
    Which *France* and *Holland* wanted power to cross:
We urge an unseen Fate to lay us low,
    And feed their envious eyes with *English* loss.   [840]

Each Element his dread command obeys,   5
    Who makes or ruines with a smile or frown;
Who as by one he did our Nation raise,
    So now he with another pulls us down.

Yet, *London*, Empress of the Northern Clime,
    By an high fate thou greatly didst expire;   10
Great as the worlds, which at the death of time
    Must fall, and rise a nobler frame by fire.

As when some dire Usurper Heav'n provides,
    To scourge his Country with a lawless sway:
His birth, perhaps, some petty Village hides,   15
    And sets his Cradle out of Fortune's way:

Till fully ripe his swelling fate breaks out,
    And hurries him to mighty mischiefs on:
His Prince surpriz'd at first, no ill could doubt,
    And wants the pow'r to meet it when 'tis known: 20

Such was the rise of this prodigious fire,
    Which in mean buildings first obscurely bred,
From thence did soon to open streets aspire,
    And straight to Palaces and Temples spread.   [860]

The diligence of Trades and noiseful gain,   25
   And luxury, more late, asleep were laid:
All was the nights, and in her silent reign,
   No sound the rest of Nature did invade.

In this deep quiet, from what source unknown,
   Those seeds of fire their fatal birth disclose: 30
And first, few scatt'ring sparks about were blown,
   Big with the flames that to our ruine rose.

Then, in some close-pent room it crept along,
   And, smouldring as it went, in silence fed:
Till th' infant monster, with devouring strong,   35
   Walk'd boldly upright with exalted head.

Now, like some rich or mighty Murderer,
   Too great for prison, which he breaks with gold:
Who fresher for new mischiefs does appear,
   And dares the world to tax him with the old: 40

So scapes th' insulting fire his narrow Jail,
   And makes small out-lets into open air:
There the fierce winds his tender force assail,
   And beat him down-ward to his first repair.   [880]

The winds, like crafty Courtezans, with-held   45
   His flames from burning, but to blow them more:
And, every fresh attempt, he is repell'd
   With faint denials, weaker then before.

And now, no longer letted of his prey,
   He leaps up at it with inrag'd desire: 50
O'r-looks the neighbours with a wide survey,
   And nods at every house his threatning fire.

The Ghosts of Traitors, from the *Bridge* descend,
  With bold Fanatick Spectres to rejoyce:
About the fire into a Dance they bend,   55
  And sing their Sabbath Notes with feeble voice.

Our Guardian Angel saw them where he sate
  Above the Palace of our slumbring King,
He sigh'd, abandoning his charge to Fate,
  And, drooping, oft lookt back upon the wing.   60

At length the crackling noise and dreadful blaze,
  Call'd up some waking Lover to the sight:
And long it was ere he the rest could raise,
  Whose heavy eye-lids yet were full of night.   [900]

The next to danger, hot pursu'd by fate,   65
  Half cloth'd, half naked, hastily retire:
And frighted Mothers strike their breasts, too late,
  For helpless Infants left amidst the fire.

Their cries soon waken all the dwellers near:
  Now murmuring noises rise in every street: 70
The more remote run stumbling with their fear,
  And, in the dark, men justle as they meet.

So weary Bees in little Cells repose:
  But if night-robbers lift the well-stor'd Hive,
An humming through their waxen City grows,   75
  And out upon each others wings they drive.

Now streets grow throng'd and busie as by day:
  Some run for Buckets to the hallow'd Quire:
Some cut the Pipes, and some the Engines play,
  And some more bold mount Ladders to the fire.   80

In vain: for, from the East, a *Belgian* wind,
  His hostile breath through the dry rafters sent:
The flames impell'd, soon left their foes behind,
  And forward, with a wanton fury went. [920]

A Key of fire ran all along the shore, 85
  And lighten'd all the River with the blaze:
The waken'd Tydes began again to roar,
  And wond'ring Fish in shining waters gaze.

Old Father *Thames* rais'd up his reverend head,
  But fear'd the fate of *Simoeis* would return: 90
Deep in his *Ooze* he sought his sedgy bed,
  And shrunk his waters back into his Urn.

The fire, mean time, walks in a broader gross,
  To either hand his wings he opens wide:
He wades the streets, and straight he reaches cross, 95
  And plays his longing flames on th' other side.

At first they warm, then scorch, and then they take:
  Now with long necks from side to side they feed:
At length, grown strong, their Mother fire forsake,
  And a new Collony of flames succeed. 100

To every nobler portion of the Town,
  The curling billows roul their restless Tyde:
In parties now they straggle up and down,
  As Armies, unoppos'd, for prey divide. [940]

One mighty Squadron, with a side wind sped, 105
  Through narrow lanes his cumber'd fire does haste:
By pow'rful charms of gold and silver led,
  The *Lombard* Banquers and the *Change* to waste.

Another backward to the *Tow'r* would go,
　　And slowly eats his way against the wind:　　　110
But the main body of the marching foe
　　Against th' Imperial Palace is design'd.

Now day appears, and with the day the King,
　　Whose early care had robb'd him of his rest:
Far off the cracks of falling houses ring,　　　115
　　And shrieks of subjects pierce his tender breast.

Near as he draws, thick harbingers of smoke,
　　With gloomy pillars, cover all the place:
Whose little intervals of night are broke
　　By sparks that drive against his Sacred Face.　　　120

More then his Guards his sorrows made him known,
　　And pious tears which down his cheeks did show'r:
The wretched in his grief forgot their own:
　　(So much the pity of a King has pow'r.)　　　[960]

He wept the flames of what he lov'd so well,　　　125
　　And what so well had merited his love.
For never Prince in grace did more excel,
　　Or Royal City more in duty strove.

Nor with an idle care did he behold:
　　(Subjects may grieve, but Monarchs must redress.)　　　130
He chears the fearful, and commends the bold,
　　And makes despairers hope for good success.

Himself directs what first is to be done,
　　And orders all the succours which they bring.
The helpful and the good about him run,　　　135
　　And form an Army worthy such a King.

He sees the dire contagion spread so fast,
   That where it seizes, all relief is vain:
And therefore must unwillingly lay waste
   That Country which would, else, the foe maintain.   140

The powder blows up all before the fire:
   Th' amazed flames stand gather'd on a heap;
And from the precipices brinck retire,
   Afraid to venture on so large a leap.   [980]

Thus fighting fires a while themselves consume,   145
   But straight, like *Turks*, forc'd on to win or die,
They first lay tender bridges of their fume,
   And o'r the breach in unctuous vapours flie.

Part stays for passage till a gust of wind
   Ships o'r their forces in a shining sheet: 150
Part, creeping under ground, their journey blind,
   And, climbing from below, their fellows meet.

Thus, to some desart plain, or old wood side,
   Dire night-hags come from far to dance their round:
And o'r brode Rivers on their fiends they ride,   155
   Or sweep in clowds above the blasted ground.

No help avails: for, *Hydra*-like, the fire,
   Lifts up his hundred heads to aim his way.
And scarce the wealthy can one half retire,
   Before he rushes in to share the prey.   160

The rich grow suppliant, and the poor grow proud:
   Those offer mighty gain, and these ask more.
So void of pity is th' ignoble crowd,
   When others ruine may increase their store.   [1000]

As those who live by shores with joy behold   165
  Some wealthy vessel split or stranded nigh;
And, from the Rocks, leap down for shipwrack'd Gold,
  And seek the Tempest which the others flie:

So these but wait the Owners last despair,
  And what's permitted to the flames invade: 170
Ev'n from their jaws they hungry morsels tear,
  And, on their backs, the spoils of *Vulcan* lade.

The days were all in this lost labour spent;
  And when the weary King gave place to night,
His Beams he to his Royal Brother lent,   175
  And so shone still in his reflective light.

Night came, but without darkness or repose,
  A dismal picture of the gen'ral doom:
Where Souls distracted when the Trumpet blows,
  And half unready with their bodies come.   180

Those who have homes, when home they do repair
  To a last lodging call their wand'ring friends.
Their short uneasie sleeps are broke with care,
  To look how near their own destruction tends.   [1020]

Those who have none sit round where once it was,   185
  And with full eyes each wonted room require:
Haunting the yet warm ashes of the place,
  As murder'd men walk where they did expire.

Some stir up coals and watch the Vestal fire,
  Others in vain from sight of ruine run: 190
And, while through burning Lab'rinths they retire,
  With loathing eyes repeat what they would shun.

The most, in fields, like herded beasts lie down;
  To dews obnoxious on the grassie floor:
And while their Babes in sleep their sorrows drown,   195
  Sad Parents watch the remnants of their store.

While by the motion of the flames they ghess
  What streets are burning now, and what are near:
An Infant, waking, to the paps would press,
  And meets, instead of milk, a falling tear.   200

No thought can ease them but their Sovereign's care,
  Whose praise th' afflicted as their comfort sing:
Ev'n those whom want might drive to just despair,
  Think life a blessing under such a King.   [1040]

Mean time he sadly suffers in their grief,   205
  Out-weeps an Hermite, and out-prays a Saint:
All the long night he studies their relief,
  How they may be suppli'd, and he may want.

O God, said he, thou Patron of my days,
  Guide of my youth in exile and distress!   210
Who me unfriended, brought'st by wondrous ways
  The Kingdom of my Fathers to possess:

King's Prayer.

Be thou my Judge, with what unwearied care
  I since have labour'd for my People's good:
To bind the bruises of a Civil War,   215
  And stop the issues of their wasting bloud.

Thou, who has taught me to forgive the ill,
  And recompense, as friends, the good misled;
If mercy be a Precept of thy will,
  Return that mercy on thy Servant's head.   220

Or, if my heedless Youth has stept astray,
    Too soon forgetful of thy gracious hand:
On me alone thy just displeasure lay,
    But take thy judgments from this mourning Land.   [1060]

We all have sinn'd, and thou hast laid us low,   225
    As humble Earth from whence at first we came:
Like flying shades before the clowds we show,
    And shrink like Parchment in consuming flame.

O let it be enough what thou hast done,
    When spotted deaths ran arm'd through every street, 230
With poison'd darts, which not the good could shun,
    The speedy could out-fly, or valiant meet.

The living few, and frequent funerals then,
    Proclam'd thy wrath on this forsaken place:
And now those few who are return'd agen   235
    Thy searching judgments to their dwellings trace.

O pass not, Lord, an absolute decree,
    Or bind thy sentence unconditional:
But in thy sentence our remorce foresee,
    And, in that foresight, this thy doom recall.   240

Thy threatnings, Lord, as thine, thou maist revoke:
    But, if immutable and fix'd they stand,
Continue still thy self to give the stroke,
    And let not foreign foes oppress thy Land.   [1080]

Th' Eternal heard, and from the Heav'nly Quire,   245
    Chose out the Cherub with the flaming sword:
And bad him swiftly drive th' approaching fire
    From where our Naval Magazins were stor'd.

The blessed Minister his wings displai'd,
   And like a shooting Star he cleft the night: 250
He charg'd the flames, and those that disobey'd,
   He lash'd to duty with his sword of light.

The fugitive flames, chastis'd, went forth to prey
   On pious Structures, by our Fathers rear'd:
By which to Heav'n they did affect the way,   255
   Ere Faith in Church-men without Works was heard.

The wanting Orphans saw, with watry eyes,
   Their Founders charity in dust laid low:
And sent to God their ever-answer'd cries,
   (For he protects the poor who made them so.)   260

Nor could thy Fabrick, *Paul*'s, defend thee long,
   Though thou wert Sacred to thy Makers praise:
Though made immortal by a Poet's Song;
   And Poets Songs the *Theban* walls could raise.   [1100]

The dareing flames peep't in and saw from far,   265
   The awful beauties of the Sacred Quire:
But, since it was prophan'd by Civil War,
   Heav'n thought it fit to have it purg'd by fire.

Now down the narrow streets it swiftly came,
   And, widely opening, did on both sides prey.   270
This benefit we sadly owe the flame,
   If onely ruine must enlarge our way.

And now four days the Sun had seen our woes,
   Four nights the Moon beheld th' incessant fire:
It seem'd as if the Stars more sickly rose,   275
   And farther from the feav'rish North retire.

In th' Empyrean Heaven, (the bless'd abode)
   The Thrones and the Dominions prostrate lie,
Not daring to behold their angry God:
   And an hush'd silence damps the tuneful sky.   280

At length th' Almighty cast a pitying eye,
   And mercy softly touch'd his melting breast:
He saw the Town's one half in rubbish lie,
   And eager flames give on to storm the rest.   [1120]

An hollow chrystal Pyramid he takes,   285
   In firmamental waters dipt above;
Of it a brode Extinguisher he makes,
   And hoods the flames that to their quarry strove.

The vanquish'd fires withdraw from every place,
   Or full with feeding, sink into a sleep: 290
Each houshold Genius shows again his face,
   And, from the hearths, the little Lares creep.

Our King this more then natural change beholds;
   With sober joy his heart and eyes abound:
To the All-good his lifted hands he folds,   295
   And thanks him low on his redeemed ground.

As when sharp frosts had long constrain'd the earth,
   A kindly thaw unlocks it with mild rain:
And first the tender blade peeps up to birth,
   And straight the green fields laugh with promis'd grain: 300

By such degrees, the spreading gladness grew
   In every heart, which fear had froze before:
The standing streets with so much joy they view,
   That with less grief the perish'd they deplore.   [1140]

The Father of the people open'd wide   305
    His stores, and all the poor with plenty fed:
Thus God's Annointed God's own place suppli'd,
    And fill'd the empty with his daily bread.

This Royal bounty brought its own reward,
    And, in their minds, so deep did print the sense: 310
That if their ruines sadly they regard,
    'Tis but with fear the sight might drive him thence.

But so may he live long, that Town to sway,
    Which by his Auspice they will nobler make,
As he will hatch their ashes by his stay,   315
    And not their humble ruines now forsake.

Cities request to the King not to leave them.

They have not lost their Loyalty by fire;
    Nor is their courage or their wealth so low,
That from his Wars they poorly would retire,
    Or beg the pity of a vanquish'd foe.   320

Not with more constancy the *Jews* of old,
    By *Cyrus* from rewarded Exile sent:
Their Royal City did in dust behold,
    Or with more vigour to rebuild it went.   [1160]

The utmost malice of their Stars is past,   325
    And two dire Comets which have scourg'd the Town,
In their own Plague and Fire have breath'd their last,
    Or, dimly, in their sinking sockets frown.

Now frequent Trines the happier lights among,
    And high-rais'd *Jove* from his dark prison freed: 330
(Those weights took off that on his Planet hung)
    Will gloriously the new laid work succeed.

Me-thinks already, from this Chymick flame,
　　I see a City of more precious mold:
Rich as the Town which gives the *Indies* name,   335
　　With Silver pav'd, and all divine with Gold.

Already, Labouring with a mighty fate,
　　She shakes the rubbish from her mounting brow,
And seems to have renew'd her Charters date,
　　Which Heav'n will to the death of time allow.   340

More great then humane, now, and more *August*,
　　New deifi'd she from her fires does rise:
Her widening streets on new foundations trust,
　　And, opening, into larger parts she flies.   [1180]

Before, she like some Shepherdess did show,   345
　　Who sate to bathe her by a River's side:
Not answering to her fame, but rude and low,
　　Nor taught the beauteous Arts of Modern pride.

Now, like a Maiden Queen, she will behold,
　　From her high Turrets, hourly Sutors come: 350
The East with Incense, and the West with Gold,
　　Will stand, like Suppliants, to receive her doom.

The silver *Thames*, her own domestick Floud,
　　Shall bear her Vessels, like a sweeping Train;
And often wind (as of his Mistress proud)   355
　　With longing eyes to meet her face again.

The wealthy *Tagus*, and the wealthier *Rhine*,
　　The glory of their Towns no more shall boast:
And *Sein*, That would with *Belgian* Rivers joyn,
　　Shall find her lustre stain'd, and Traffick lost.   360

The vent'rous Merchant, who design'd more far,
　　And touches on our hospitable shore:
Charm'd with the splendour of this Northern Star,
　　Shall here unlade him, and depart no more.　　　[1200]

Our pow'rful Navy shall no longer meet,　　　　　365
　　The wealth of *France* or *Holland* to invade:
The beauty of this Town, without a Fleet,
　　From all the world shall vindicate her Trade.

And, while this fam'd Emporium we prepare,
　　The *British* Ocean shall such triumphs boast,　　370
That those who now disdain our Trade to share,
　　Shall rob like Pyrats on our wealthy Coast.

Already we have conquer'd half the War,
　　And the less dang'rous part is left behind:
Our trouble now is but to make them dare,　　　375
　　And not so great to vanquish as to find.

Thus to the Eastern wealth through storms we go;
　　But now, the Cape once doubled, fear no more:
A constant Trade-wind will securely blow,
　　And gently lay us on the Spicy shore.　　　　380

Baucis and Philemon, out of the Eighth Book of Ovid's Metamorphoses

Fables (1700)

THEN *Lelex* rose, an old experienc'd Man,
And thus with sober Gravity began:
Heav'ns Pow'r is Infinite: Earth, Air, and Sea,
The Manufacture Mass, the making Pow'r obey:

By Proof to clear your Doubt; In *Phrygian* Ground   5
Two neighb'ring Trees, with Walls encompass'd round,
Stand on a mod'rate Rise, with wonder shown,
One a hard Oak, a softer Linden one:
I saw the Place and them, by *Pittheus* sent
To *Phrygian* Realms, my Grandsire's Government.   10 [20]
Not far from thence is seen a Lake, the Haunt
Of Coots, and of the fishing Cormorant:
Here *Jove* with *Hermes* came; but in Disguise
Of mortal Men conceal'd their Deities;
One laid aside his Thunder, one his Rod;   15
And many toilsom Steps together trod:
For Harbour at a thousand Doors they knock'd,
Not one of all the thousand but was lock'd.
At last an hospitable House they found,
A homely Shed; the Roof, not far from Ground,   20
Was thatch'd with Reeds, and Straw together bound.
There *Baucis* and *Philemon* liv'd, and there
Had liv'd long marry'd, and a happy Pair:
Now old in Love, though little was their Store,
Inur'd to Want, their Poverty they bore,   25
Nor aim'd at Wealth, professing to be poor.
For Master or for Servant here to call,
Was all alike, where only Two were All.
Command was none, where equal Love was paid,
Or rather both commanded, both obey'd.   30 [40]
    From lofty Roofs the Gods repuls'd before,
Now stooping, enter'd through the little Door:
The Man (their hearty Welcome first express'd)
A common Settle drew for either Guest,
Inviting each his weary Limbs to rest.   35
But e'er they sat, officious *Baucis* lays
Two Cushions stuff'd with Straw, the Seat to raise;

Course, but the best she had; then rakes the Load
Of Ashes from the Hearth, and spreads abroad
The living Coals; and, lest they shou'd expire,   40
With Leaves and Barks she feeds her Infant-fire:
It smoaks; and then with trembling Breath she blows,
Till in a chearful Blaze the Flames arose.
With Brush-wood and with Chips she strengthens these,
And adds at last the Boughs of rotten Trees.   45
The Fire thus form'd, she sets the Kettle on,
(Like burnish'd Gold the little Seether shone)
Next took the Coleworts which her Husband got
From his own Ground, (a small well-water'd Spot;)
She stripp'd the Stalks of all their Leaves; the best   50 [60]
She cull'd, and then with handy-care she dress'd.
High o'er the Hearth a Chine of Bacon hung;
Good old *Philemon* seiz'd it with a Prong,
And from the sooty Rafter drew it down,
Then cut a Slice, but scarce enough for one;   55
Yet a large Portion of a little Store,
Which for their Sakes alone he wish'd were more.
This in the Pot he plung'd without delay,
To tame the Flesh, and drain the Salt away.
The Time between, before the Fire they sat,   60
And shorten'd the Delay by pleasing Chat.

   A Beam there was, on which a Beechen Pail
Hung by the Handle, on a driven Nail:
This fill'd with Water, gently warm'd, they set ⎫
Before their Guests; in this they bath'd their Feet, ⎬   65
And after with clean Towels dry'd their Sweat: ⎭
This done, the Host produc'd the genial Bed, ⎫
Sallow the Feet, the Borders, and the Sted, ⎬
Which with no costly Coverlet they spread; ⎭
But course old Garments, yet such Robes as these   70 [80]

They laid alone, at Feasts, on Holydays.
The good old Huswife tucking up her Gown,
The Table sets; th' invited Gods lie down.
The Trivet-Table of a Foot was lame,
A Blot which prudent *Baucis* overcame,   75
Who thrusts beneath the limping Leg, a Sherd,
So was the mended Board exactly rear'd:
Then rubb'd it o'er with newly-gather'd Mint,
A wholesom Herb, that breath'd a grateful Scent.
Pallas began the Feast, where first was seen   80
The party-colour'd Olive, Black, and Green:
Autumnal Cornels next in order serv'd,
In Lees of Wine well pickl'd, and preserv'd.
A Garden-Sallad was the third Supply,
Of Endive, Radishes, and Succory: 85
Then Curds and Cream, the Flow'r of Country-Fare,⎫
And new-laid Eggs, which *Baucis* busie Care   ⎬
Turn'd by a gentle Fire, and roasted rear.   ⎭
All these in Earthen Ware were serv'd to Board; ⎫
And next in place, an Earthen Pitcher stor'd   ⎬   90 [100]
With Liquor of the best the Cottage cou'd afford.⎭
This was the Tables Ornament, and Pride,
With Figures wrought: Like Pages at his Side
Stood Beechen Bowls; and these were shining clean,
Vernish'd with Wax without, and lin'd within.   95
By this the boiling Kettle had prepar'd,
And to the Table sent the smoaking Lard;
On which with eager Appetite they dine,
A sav'ry Bit, that serv'd to rellish Wine:
The Wine it self was suiting to the rest,   100
Still working in the Must, and lately press'd.
The Second Course succeeds like that before,
Plums, Apples, Nuts, and of their Wintry Store,

Dry Figs, and Grapes, and wrinkl'd Dates were set
In Canisters, t' enlarge the little Treat: 105
All these a Milk-white Honey-comb surround,
Which in the midst the Country-Banquet crown'd:
But the kind Hosts their Entertainment grace
With hearty Welcom, and an open Face:
In all they did, you might discern with ease,   110 [120]
A willing Mind, and a Desire to please.

   Mean time the Beechen Bowls went round, and still
Though often empty'd, were observ'd to fill;
Fill'd without Hands, and of their own accord
Ran without Feet, and danc'd about the Board.   115
Devotion seiz'd the Pair, to see the Feast
With Wine, and of no common Grape, increas'd;
And up they held their Hands, and fell to Pray'r,
Excusing as they cou'd, their Country Fare.

   One Goose they had, ('twas all they cou'd allow)   120
A wakeful Cent'ry, and on Duty now,
Whom to the Gods for Sacrifice they vow:
Her, with malicious Zeal, the Couple view'd;
She ran for Life, and limping they pursu'd:
Full well the Fowl perceiv'd their bad intent,   125
And wou'd not make her Masters Compliment;
But persecuted, to the Pow'rs she flies,
And close between the Legs of *Jove* she lies:
He with a gracious Ear the Suppliant heard,
And sav'd her Life; then what he was declar'd,   130 [140]
And own'd the God. The Neighbourhood, said he,
Shall justly perish for Impiety:
You stand alone exempted; but obey
With speed, and follow where we lead the way:
Leave these accurs'd; and to the Mountains Height   135
Ascend; nor once look backward in your Flight.

They haste, and what their tardy Feet deny'd,
The trusty Staff (their better Leg) supply'd.
An Arrows Flight they wanted to the Top,
And there secure, but spent with Travel, stop;   140
Then turn their now no more forbidden Eyes;
Lost in a Lake the floated Level lies:
A Watry Desart covers all the Plains,
Their Cot alone, as in an Isle, remains:
Wondring with weeping Eyes, while they deplore   145
Their Neighbours Fate, and Country now no more,
Their little Shed, scarce large enough for Two,
Seems, from the Ground increas'd, in Height and Bulk to
    grow.
A stately Temple shoots within the Skies,
The Crotches of their Cot in Columns rise: 150 [160]
The Pavement polish'd Marble they behold,
The Gates with Sculpture grac'd, the Spires and Tiles of Gold.
    Then thus the Sire of Gods, with Look serene,
Speak thy Desire, thou only Just of Men;
And thou, O Woman, only worthy found   155
To be with such a Man in Marriage bound.
    A while they whisper; then to *Jove* address'd,
Philemon thus prefers their joint Request.
We crave to serve before your sacred Shrine,
And offer at your Altars Rites Divine: 160
And since not any Action of our Life
Has been polluted with Domestick Strife,
We beg one Hour of Death; that neither she
With Widows Tears may live to bury me,
Nor weeping I, with wither'd Arms may bear   165
My breathless *Baucis* to the Sepulcher.
    The Godheads sign their Suit. They run their Race
In the same Tenor all th' appointed Space:

Then, when their Hour was come, while they relate
These past Adventures at the Temple-gate,   170 [180]
Old *Baucis* is by old *Philemon* seen
Sprouting with sudden Leaves of spritely Green:
Old *Baucis* look'd where old *Philemon* stood,
And saw his lengthen'd Arms a sprouting Wood:
New Roots their fasten'd Feet begin to bind,   175
Their Bodies stiffen in a rising Rind:
Then e'er the Bark above their Shoulders grew,
They give and take at once their last Adieu:
At once, Farewell, O faithful Spouse, they said;
At once th' incroaching Rinds their closing Lips invade.   180
Ev'n yet, an ancient *Tyanæan* shows
A spreading Oak, that near a Linden grows;
The Neighbourhood confirm the Prodigie,
Grave Men, not vain of Tongue, or like to lie.
I saw my self the Garlands on their Boughs,   185
And Tablets hung for Gifts of granted Vows;
And off'ring fresher up, with pious Pray'r,
The Good, said I, are God's peculiar Care,
And such as honour Heav'n, shall heav'nly Honour share.

From The Twelfth Book of Ovid His Metamorphoses

Fables (1700)

Now brave *Perithous*, bold *Ixion*'s Son,
The Love of fair *Hippodame* had won.
The Cloud-begotten Race half Men, half Beast,
Invited, came to grace the Nuptial Feast:
In a cool Cave's recess, the Treat was made,   5
Whose entrance, Trees with spreading Boughs o'ershade.

They sate: And summon'd by the Bridegroom, came
To mix with those the *Lapythæan* Name:
Nor wanted I: The Roofs with Joy resound: [300]
And *Hymen*, *Io Hymen*, rung around.   10
Rais'd Altars shone with holy Fires; the Bride,
Lovely her self (and lovely by her side
A bevy of bright Nimphs, with sober Grace,)
Came glitt'ring like a Star; and took her Place.
Her heav'nly Form beheld, all wish'd her Joy;   15
And little wanted, but in vain, their Wishes all employ.

  For One, most Brutal, of the Brutal Brood,
Or whether Wine or Beauty fir'd his Blood,
Or both at once; beheld with lustful Eyes
The Bride; at once resolv'd to make his Prize.   20
Down went the Board; and fastning on her Hair,
He seiz'd with sudden Force the frighted Fair.
'Twas *Eurytus* began: His bestial Kind
His Crime pursu'd; and each as pleas'd his Mind,
Or her, whom Chance presented, took: The Feast   25
An Image of a taken Town express'd.

  The Cave resounds with Female Shrieks; we rise,
Mad with Revenge, to make a swift Reprise:
And *Theseus* first; what Frenzy has possess'd   [320]
O *Eurytus*, he cry'd, thy brutal Breast,   30
To wrong *Perithous*, and not him alone,
But while I live, two Friends conjoyn'd in one?

  To justify his Threat, he thrusts aside
The Crowd of Centaurs; and redeems the Bride:
The Monster nought reply'd: For Words were vain;   35
And Deeds cou'd only Deeds unjust maintain:
But answers with his Hand; and forward press'd,
With Blows redoubled, on his Face and Breast.
An ample Goblet stood, of antick Mold,

And rough with Figures of the rising Gold;   40
The Hero snatch'd it up: And toss'd in Air,
Full at the Front of the foul Ravisher.
He falls; and falling vomits forth a Flood
Of Wine, and Foam and Brains, and mingled Blood.
Half roaring, and half neighing through the Hall,   45
Arms, Arms, the double form'd with Fury call;
To wreak their Brother's death: A Medley-Flight
Of Bowls and Jars, at first supply the Fight.
Once Instruments of Feasts; but now of Fate;   [340]
Wine animates their Rage, and arms their Hate.   50
   Bold *Amycus*, from the robb'd Vestry brings
The Chalices of Heav'n; and holy Things
Of precious Weight: A Sconce, that hung on high,
With Tapers fill'd, to light the Sacristy,
Torn from the Cord, with his unhallow'd Hand   55
He threw amid the *Lapythæan* Band.
On *Celadon* the Ruin fell; and left
His Face of Feature and of Form bereft:
So, when some brawny Sacrificer knocks
Before an Altar led, an offer'd Oxe,   60
His Eye-balls rooted out, are thrown to Ground; ⎞
His Nose dismantled, in his Mouth is found,   ⎬
His Jaws, Cheeks, Front, one undistinguish'd Wound. ⎠

                  *   *   *   *

   Nor cou'd thy Form, O *Cyllarus*, foreslow
Thy Fate; (if Form to Monsters Men allow:)   65
Just bloom'd thy Beard: Thy Beard of golden Hew:
Thy Locks in golden Waves, about thy Shoulders flew.
Sprightly thy Look: Thy Shapes in ev'ry part
So clean, as might instruct the Sculptor's Art;
As far as Man extended: Where began   70 [530]
The Beast, the Beast was equal to the Man.

Add but a Horses Head and Neck; and he,
O *Castor*, was a Courser worthy thee.
So was his Back proportion'd for the Seat;
So rose his brawny Chest; so swiftly mov'd his Feet.   75
Coal-black his Colour, but like Jet it shone;
His Legs and flowing Tail, were White alone.
Belov'd by many Maidens of his Kind;
But fair *Hylonome*, possess'd his Mind:
Hylonome, for Features, and for Face   80
Excelling all the Nymphs of double Race:
Nor less her Blandishments, than Beauty move;
At once both loving, and confessing Love.
For him she dress'd: For him with Female Care
She comb'd, and set in Curls, her auburn Hair.   85
Of Roses, Violets, and Lillies mix'd
And Sprigs of flowing Rosemary betwixt
She form'd the Chaplet, that adorn'd her Front:
In Waters of the *Pagasæan* Fount,
And in the Streams that from the Fountain play,   90 [550]
She wash'd her Face; and bath'd her twice a Day.
The Scarf of Furs, that hung below her Side,
Was Ermin, or the Panther's spotted Pride;
Spoils of no common Beast: With equal Flame
They lov'd: Their *Sylvan* Pleasures were the same: 95
All Day they hunted: And when Day expir'd,
Together to some shady Cave retir'd:
Invited to the Nuptials, both repair:
And Side by Side, they both ingage in War.

Uncertain from what Hand, a flying Dart   100
At *Cyllarus* was sent; which pierc'd his Heart.
The Javelin drawn from out the mortal Wound,
He faints with staggring Steps; and seeks the Ground:
The Fair, within her Arms receiv'd his fall,

And strove his wandring Spirits to recal: 105
And while her Hand the streaming Blood oppos'd,
Join'd Face to Face, his Lips with hers she clos'd.
Stifled with Kisses, a sweet Death he dies;
She fills the Fields with undistinguish'd Cries:
At least her Words, were in her Clamour drown'd; 110 [570]
For my stun'd Ears receiv'd no vocal Sound.
In madness of her Grief, she seiz'd the Dart
New-drawn, and reeking from her Lover's Heart;
To her bare Bosom the sharp Point apply'd; ⎫
And wounded fell; and falling by his Side, ⎬ 115
Embrac'd him in her Arms; and thus embracing, dy'd. ⎭

The Fable of Acis, Polyphemus, and Galatea. From the Thirteenth Book of the Metamorphoses

Examen Poeticum (1693)

GALATEA *relates the Story*

ACIS, the Lovely Youth, whose loss I mourn,
From *Faunus* and the Nymph *Symethis* born,
Was both his Parents pleasure: but, to me
Was all that Love cou'd make a Lover be.
The Gods our Minds in mutual Bands did joyn; 5
I was his only Joy, as he was mine.
Now sixteen Summers the sweet Youth had seen;
And doubtful Down, began to shade his Chin:
When *Polyphemus* first disturb'd our Joy;
And lov'd me fiercely, as I lov'd the Boy. 10
Ask not which passion in my Soul was high'r,
My last Aversion, or my first Desire:

Nor this the greater was, nor that the less:
Both were alike; for both were in excess.
Thee, *Venus*, thee, both Heav'n and Earth obey;   15
Immense thy Pow'r, and boundless is thy Sway.
The *Cyclops*, who defi'd th' Ætherial Throne,
And thought no Thunder louder than his own,
The terrour of the Woods, and wilder far
Than Wolves in Plains, or Bears in Forrests are,   20
Th' Inhumane Host, who made his bloody Feasts
On mangl'd Members, of his butcher'd Guests,
Yet felt the force of Love, and fierce Desire,
And burnt for me, with unrelenting Fire.
Forgot his Caverns, and his woolly care,   25
Assum'd the softness of a Lover's Air;
And comb'd, with Teeth of Rakes, his rugged hair.
Now with a crooked Sythe his Beard he sleeks;
And mows the stubborn Stubble of his Cheeks:
Now, in the Crystal Stream he looks, to try   30
His Simagres, and rowls his glaring eye.
His Cruelty and thirst of Blood are lost;
And Ships securely sail along the Coast.
    The Prophet *Telemus* (arriv'd by chance
Where *Ætna*'s Summets to the Seas advance,   35
Who mark'd the Tracts of every Bird that flew,
And sure Presages from their flying drew,)
Foretold the *Cyclops*, that *Ulysses* hand
In his broad eye, shou'd thrust a flaming Brand.
The Giant, with a scornful grin reply'd,   40
Vain Augur, thou hast falsely prophesi'd;
Already Love, his flaming Brand has tost;
Looking on two fair Eyes, my sight I lost.
Thus, warn'd in vain, with stalking pace he strode,
And stamp'd the Margine of the briny Flood,   45

With heavy steps: and weary, sought agen,
The cool Retirement of his gloomy Den.
  A Promontory sharp'ning by degrees,
Ends in a Wedge, and over-looks the Seas:
On either side, below, the water flows;   50
This airy walk, the Giant Lover chose.
Here, on the midst he sate: his Flocks, unled,
Their Shepherd follow'd, and securely fed.
A Pine so burly, and of length so vast,
That sailing Ships requir'd it for a Mast,   55
He weilded for a Staff; his steps to guide:
But laid it by, his Whistle while he try'd.
A hundred Reeds, of a prodigious growth,
Scarce made a Pipe, proportion'd to his mouth:
Which, when he gave it wind, the Rocks around,   60
And watry Plains, the dreadful hiss resound.
I heard the Ruffian-Shepherd rudely blow
Where, in a hollow Cave, I sat below;
On *Acis* bosom I my head reclin'd:
And still preserve the Poem in my mind.   65
  Oh lovely *Galatea*, whiter far
Than falling Snows, and rising Lillies are;
More flowry than the Meads, as Crystal bright,
Erect as Alders, and of equal height:
More wanton than a Kid, more sleek thy Skin   70
Than Orient Shells, that on the Shores are seen.
Than Apples fairer, when the boughs they lade,
Pleasing as Winter Suns or Summer Shade:
More grateful to the sight, than goodly Planes;
And softer to the touch, than down of Swans;   75
Or Curds new turn'd: and sweeter to the taste
Than swelling Grapes, that to the Vintage haste:
More clear than Ice, or running Streams, that stray

Through Garden Plots, but ah more swift than they.
   Yet, *Galatea*, harder to be broke,   80
Than Bullocks, unreclaim'd to bear the Yoke,
And far more stubborn, than the knotted Oak:
Like sliding Streams, impossible to hold;
Like them fallacious, like their Fountains cold.
More warping than the Willow, to decline   85
My warm Embrace, more brittle than the Vine;
Immoveable and fixt in thy disdain;
Rough as these Rocks, and of a harder grain.
More violent than is the rising Flood;
And the prais'd Peacock is not half so proud.   90
Fierce as the Fire, and sharp as Thistles are,
And more outragious than a Mother-Bear:
Deaf as the billows to the Vows I make;
And more revengeful, than a trodden Snake.
In swiftness fleeter, than the flying Hind;   95
Or driven Tempests, or the driving Wind.
All other faults, with patience I can bear;
But swiftness is the Vice I only fear.
   Yet if you knew me well, you wou'd not shun
My Love, but to my wish'd Embraces run: 100
Wou'd languish in your turn, and court my stay;
And much repent of your unwise delay.
   My Palace, in the living Rock, is made
By Nature's hand; a spacious pleasing Shade;
Which neither heat can pierce, nor cold invade.   105
My Garden fill'd with Fruits you may behold,
And Grapes in clusters, imitating Gold;
Some blushing Bunches of a purple hue:
And these and those, are all reserv'd for you.
Red Strawberries, in shades, expecting stand,   110
Proud to be gather'd by so white a hand.

Autumnal Cornels, latter Fruit provide;
And Plumbs to tempt you, turn their glossy side:
Not those of common kinds; but such alone
As in *Phæacian* Orchards might have grown: 115
Nor Chestnuts shall be wanting to your Food,
Nor Garden-fruits, nor Wildings of the Wood;
The laden Boughs for you alone shall bear;
And yours shall be the product of the Year.

  The Flocks you see, are all my own; beside ⎞   120
The rest that Woods, and winding Vallies hide; ⎬
And those that folded in the Caves abide.   ⎠
Ask not the numbers of my growing Store;
Who knows how many, knows he has no more.
Nor will I praise my Cattel, trust not me;   125
But judge your self, and pass your own decree:
Behold their swelling Dugs; the sweepy weight
Of Ews that sink beneath the Milky fraight;
In the warm Folds, their tender Lambkins lye;
Apart from Kids, that call with humane cry.   130
New Milk in Nut-brown Bowls, is duely serv'd
For daily Drink; the rest for Cheese reserv'd.
Nor are these House-hold Dainties all my Store: ⎞
The Fields and Forrests will afford us more;   ⎬
The Deer, the Hare, the Goat, the Salvage Boar, ⎠ 135
All sorts of Ven'son; and of Birds the best;
A pair of Turtles taken from the Nest.
I walk'd the Mountains, and two Cubs I found,
(Whose Dam had left 'em on the naked ground,)
So like, that no distinction cou'd be seen: 140
So pretty, they were Presents for a Queen;
And so they shall; I took 'em both away;
And keep, to be Companions of your Play.
  Oh raise, fair Nymph, your Beauteous Face above

The Waves; nor scorn my Presents, and my Love.   145
Come, *Galatea*, come, and view my face;⎫
I late beheld it, in the watry Glass;   ⎬
And found it lovelier than I fear'd it was.⎭
Survey my towring Stature, and my Size:
Not *Jove*, the *Jove* you dream that rules the Skies,   150
Bears such a bulk, or is so largely spread:
My Locks, (the plenteous Harvest of my head)
Hang o're my Manly Face; and dangling down
As with a shady Grove, my shoulders crown.
Nor think, because my limbs and body bear   155
A thick set underwood of bristling hair,
My shape deform'd; what fouler sight can be
Than the bald Branches of a leafless Tree?
Foul is the Steed, without a flowing Main:
And Birds without their Feathers and their Train.   160
Wool decks the Sheep; and Man receives a Grace
From bushy Limbs, and from a bearded Face.
My forehead, with a single eye is fill'd,
Round as a Ball, and ample as a Shield.
The Glorious Lamp of Heav'n, the Radiant Sun   165
Is Nature's eye; and she's content with one.
Add, that my Father sways your Seas, and I
Like you am of the watry Family.
I make you his, in making you my own;
You I adore; and kneel to you alone: 170
Jove, with his Fabled Thunder I despise,
And only fear the lightning of your eyes.
Frown not, fair Nymph; yet I cou'd bear to be
Disdain'd, if others were disdain'd with me.
But to repulse the *Cyclops*, and prefer   175
The Love of *Acis*, (Heav'ns) I cannot bear.
But let the Stripling please himself; nay more,

Please you, tho' that's the thing I most abhor;
The Boy shall find, if e're we cope in Fight,
These Giant Limbs, endu'd with Giant Might.   180
His living Bowels, from his Belly torn,
And scatter'd Limbs, shall on the Flood be born:
Thy Flood, ungrateful Nymph, and fate shall find
That way for thee, and *Acis* to be joyn'd.
For oh I burn with Love, and thy Disdain   185
Augments at once my Passion, and my pain.
Translated *Ætna* flames within my Heart,
And thou, Inhumane, wilt not ease my smart.

   Lamenting thus in vain, he rose, and strode
With furious paces to the Neighb'ring Wood: 190
Restless his feet, distracted was his walk;
Mad were his motions, and confus'd his talk.
Mad as the vanquish'd Bull, when forc'd to yield
His lovely Mistress, and forsake the Field.

   Thus far unseen I saw: when fatal chance   195
His looks directing, with a sudden glance,
Acis and I, were to his sight betray'd;
Where nought suspecting we securely play'd.
From his wide mouth, a bellowing cry he cast,
I see, I see; but this shall be your last: 200
A roar so loud made *Ætna* to rebound;
And all the *Cyclops* labour'd in the sound.
Affrighted with his monstrous Voice, I fled,
And in the Neighb'ring Ocean, plung'd my head.
Poor *Acis* turn'd his back, and help, he cry'd;   205
Help, *Galatea*, help, my Parent Gods,
And take me dying, to your deep Abodes.
The *Cyclops* follow'd: but he sent before
A Rib, which from the living Rock he tore:
Though but an Angle reach'd him of the Stone,   210

The mighty Fragment was enough alone
To crush all *Acis*; 'twas too late to save,
But what the Fates allow'd to give, I gave:
That *Acis* to his Lineage should return;
And rowl, among the River Gods, his Urn.   215
Straight issu'd from the Stone, a Stream of blood;
Which lost the Purple, mingling with the Flood.
Then, like a troubl'd Torrent, it appear'd:
The Torrent too, in little space was clear'd.
The Stone was cleft, and through the yawning chink,   220
New Reeds arose on the new River's brink.
The Rock, from out its hollow Womb, disclos'd
A sound like Water in its course oppos'd.
When, (wondrous to behold,) full in the Flood,
Up starts a Youth, and Navel high he stood.   225
Horns from his Temples rise; and either Horn
Thick Wreaths of Reeds, (his Native growth) adorn.
Were not his Stature taller than before,
His bulk augmented, and his beauty more,
His colour blue, for *Acis* he might pass: 230
And *Acis* chang'd into a Stream he was.
But mine no more; he rowls along the Plains
With rapid motion, and his Name retains.

From The First Book of the Georgics

The Works of Virgil (1697)

Now sing we stormy Stars, when Autumn weighs⎫
The Year, and adds to Nights, and shortens Days; ⎬   [420]
And Suns declining shine with feeble Rays: ⎭
What Cares must then attend the toiling Swain;
Or when the low'ring Spring, with lavish Rain,   5

Beats down the slender Stem and bearded Grain:
While yet the Head is green, or lightly swell'd
With Milky-moisture, over-looks the Field.
Ev'n when the Farmer, now secure of Fear,
Sends in the Swains to spoil the finish'd Year: 10
Ev'n while the Reaper fills his greedy hands,
And binds the golden Sheafs in brittle bands:
Oft have I seen a sudden Storm arise,
From all the warring Winds that sweep the Skies:
The heavy Harvest from the Root is torn,   15
And whirl'd aloft the lighter Stubble born;
With such a force the flying rack is driv'n;
And such a Winter wears the face of Heav'n:
And oft whole sheets descend of slucy Rain,
Suck'd by the spongy Clouds from off the Main: 20
The lofty Skies at once come pouring down,
The promis'd Crop and golden Labours drown.   [440]
The Dykes are fill'd, and with a roaring sound
The rising Rivers float the nether ground;
And Rocks the bellowing Voice of boiling Seas rebound. } 25
The Father of the Gods his Glory shrowds,
Involv'd in Tempests, and a Night of Clouds.
And from the middle Darkness flashing out,
By fits he deals his fiery Bolts about.
Earth feels the Motions of her angry God,   30
Her Entrails tremble, and her Mountains nod;
And flying Beasts in Forests seek abode:
Deep horrour seizes ev'ry Humane Breast,
Their Pride is humbled, and their Fear confess'd:
While he from high his rowling Thunder throws,   35
And fires the Mountains with repeated blows:
The Rocks are from their old Foundations rent;
The Winds redouble, and the Rains augment:

The Waves on heaps are dash'd against the Shoar,
And now the Woods, and now the Billows roar.   40

From The Third Book of the Æneis

The Works of Virgil (1697)

FROM *Ithaca* my native Soil I came
To *Troy*, and *Achæmenides* my Name.
Me, my poor Father, with *Ulysses* sent;
(Oh had I stay'd, with Poverty content!)
But fearful for themselves, my Country-men   5
Left me forsaken in the *Cyclops* Den.
The Cave, though large, was dark, the dismal Flore   [810]
Was pav'd with mangled Limbs and putrid Gore.
Our monstrous Host, of more than Human Size,
Erects his Head, and stares within the Skies.   10
Bellowing his Voice, and horrid is his Hue.
Ye Gods, remove this Plague from Mortal View!
The Joints of slaughter'd Wretches are his Food:
And for his Wine he quaffs the streaming Blood.
These Eyes beheld, when with his spacious Hand   15
He seiz'd two Captives of our *Grecian* Band;
Stretch'd on his Back, he dash'd against the Stones
Their broken Bodies, and their crackling Bones:
With spouting Blood the Purple Pavement swims,
While the dire Glutton grinds the trembling Limbs.   20
  Not unreveng'd, *Ulysses* bore their Fate,
Nor thoughtless of his own unhappy State:
For, gorg'd with Flesh, and drunk with Human Wine,
While fast asleep the Gyant lay supine;
Snoaring aloud, and belching from his Maw   25
His indigested Foam, and Morsels raw:

We pray, we cast the Lots, and then surround   [830]
The monstrous Body, stretch'd along the Ground:
Each, as he cou'd approach him, lends a hand
To bore his Eyeball with a flaming Brand.   30
Beneath his frowning Forehead lay his Eye,
(For onely one did the vast Frame supply;)
But that a Globe so large, his Front it fill'd,
Like the Sun's disk, or like a *Grecian* Shield.
The Stroke succeeds; and down the Pupil bends;   35
This Vengeance follow'd for our slaughter'd Friends.
But haste, unhappy Wretches, haste to fly;
Your Cables cut, and on your Oars rely.
Such, and so vast as *Polypheme* appears,
A hundred more this hated Island bears: 40
Like him in Caves they shut their woolly Sheep,   ⎫
Like him, their Herds on tops of Mountains keep;   ⎬
Like him, with mighty Strides, they stalk from Steep to Steep. ⎭
And now three Moons their sharpen'd Horns renew,
Since thus in Woods and Wilds, obscure from view,   45
I drag my loathsom Days with mortal Fright;
And in deserted Caverns lodge by Night.   [850]
Oft from the Rocks a dreadful Prospect see,
Of the huge *Cyclops*, like a walking Tree:
From far I hear his thund'ring Voice resound;   50
And trampling Feet that shake the solid Ground.
Cornels, and salvage Berries of the Wood,
And Roots and Herbs have been my meagre Food.
    While all around my longing Eyes I cast,
I saw your happy Ships appear at last.   55
On those I fix'd my hopes, to these I run,
'Tis all I ask this cruel Race to shun:
What other Death you please your selves, bestow.
Scarce had he said, when on the Mountain's brow,

We saw the Gyant-Shepherd stalk before   60
His following Flock, and leading to the Shore.
A monstrous Bulk, deform'd, depriv'd of Sight,
His Staff a trunk of Pine, to guide his steps aright.
His pondrous Whistle from his Neck descends;
His woolly Care their pensive Lord attends: 65
This onely Solace his hard Fortune sends.

Soon as he reach'd the Shore, and touch'd the Waves,   [870]
From his bor'd Eye the gutt'ring Blood he laves:
He gnash'd his Teeth and groan'd; thro' Seas he strides,
And scarce the topmost Billows touch'd his sides.   70
    Seiz'd with a sudden Fear, we run to Sea,
The Cables cut, and silent haste away:
The well deserving Stranger entertain;
Then, buckling to the Work, our Oars divide the Main.
The Gyant harken'd to the dashing Sound: 75
But when our Vessels out of reach he found,
He strided onward; and in vain essay'd
Th' *Ionian* Deep, and durst no farther wade.
With that he roar'd aloud; the dreadful Cry
Shakes Earth, and Air, and Seas; the Billows fly   80
Before the bellowing Noise, to distant *Italy*.
The neighb'ring *Ætna* trembled all around;
The winding Caverns echo to the sound.
His brother *Cyclops* hear the yelling Roar;
And, rushing down the Mountains, crowd the Shoar: 85
We saw their stern distorted looks, from far,
And one ey'd Glance, that vainly threatned War.   [890]
A dreadful Council, with their heads on high;
The misty Clouds about their Foreheads fly:
Not yielding to the tow'ring Tree of *Jove*;   90
Or tallest Cypress of *Diana*'s Grove.
New Pangs of mortal Fear our Minds assail,

We tug at ev'ry Oar, and hoist up ev'ry Sail;
And take th' Advantage of the friendly Gale.

From The Sixth Book of the Æneis

The Works of Virgil (1697)

YE Realms, yet unreveal'd to human sight,   1
Ye Gods, who rule the Regions of the Night,
Ye gliding Ghosts, permit me to relate
The mystick Wonders of your silent State.
   Obscure they went thro dreery Shades, that led   5
Along the waste Dominions of the dead:
Thus wander Travellers in Woods by Night,   [380]
By the Moon's doubtful, and malignant Light:
When *Jove* in dusky Clouds involves the Skies;
And the faint Crescent shoots by fits before their Eyes.   10
   Just in the Gate, and in the Jaws of Hell,
Revengeful Cares, and sullen Sorrows dwell;
And pale Diseases, and repining Age;
Want, Fear, and Famine's unresisted rage.
Here Toils, and Death, and Death's half-brother, Sleep,   15
Forms terrible to view, their Centry keep:
With anxious Pleasures of a guilty Mind,
Deep Frauds before, and open Force behind:
The Furies Iron Beds, and Strife that shakes
Her hissing Tresses, and unfolds her Snakes.   20
Full in the midst of this infernal Road,
An Elm displays her dusky Arms abroad;
The God of Sleep there hides his heavy Head:
And empty Dreams on ev'ry Leaf are spread.
Of various Forms unnumber'd Specters more;   25
Centaurs, and double Shapes, besiege the Door:

Before the Passage horrid *Hydra* stands,   [400]
And *Briareus* with all his hundred Hands:
Gorgons, Geryon with his triple Frame;
And vain *Chimæra* vomits empty Flame.   30
The Chief unsheath'd his shining Steel, prepar'd,
Tho seiz'd with sudden Fear, to force the Guard.
Off'ring his brandish'd Weapon at their Face;
Had not the Sibyl stop'd his eager Pace,
And told him what those empty Fantomes were;   35
Forms without Bodies, and impassive Air.
Hence to deep *Acheron* they take their way;
Whose troubled Eddies, thick with Ooze and Clay,
Are whirl'd aloft, and in *Cocytus* lost:
There *Charon* stands, who rules the dreary Coast: 40
A sordid God; down from his hoary Chin
A length of Beard descends; uncomb'd, unclean:
His Eyes, like hollow Furnaces on Fire:
A Girdle, foul with grease, binds his obscene Attire.
He spreads his Canvas, with his Pole he steers;   45
The Freights of flitting Ghosts in his thin Bottom bears.
He look'd in Years; yet in his Years were seen   [420]
A youthful Vigour, and Autumnal green.
An Airy Crowd came rushing where he stood;
Which fill'd the Margin of the fatal Flood.   50
Husbands and Wives, Boys and unmarry'd Maids;
And mighty Heroes more Majestick Shades.
And Youths, intomb'd before their Fathers Eyes,
With hollow Groans, and Shrieks, and feeble Cries:
Thick as the Leaves in Autumn strow the Woods: 55
Or Fowls, by Winter forc'd, forsake the Floods,
And wing their hasty flight to happier Lands: ⎫
Such, and so thick, the shiv'ring Army stands: ⎬
And press for passage with extended hands.   ⎭

Cymon and Iphigenia, from Boccace

Fables (1700)

POETA LOQUITUR,

OLD as I am, for Ladies Love unfit,
The Pow'r of Beauty I remember yet,
Which once inflam'd my Soul, and still inspires my Wit.
If Love be Folly, the severe Divine
Has felt that Folly, tho' he censures mine;   5
Pollutes the Pleasures of a chast Embrace,
Acts what I write, and propagates in Grace
With riotous Excess, a Priestly Race:
Suppose him free, and that I forge th' Offence,
He shew'd the way, perverting first my Sense: 10
In Malice witty, and with Venom fraught,
He makes me speak the Things I never thought.
Compute the Gains of his ungovern'd Zeal;
Ill sutes his Cloth the Praise of Railing well!
The World will think that what we loosly write,   15
Tho' now arraign'd, he read with some delight;
Because he seems to chew the Cud again,
When his broad Comment makes the Text too plain:
And teaches more in one explaining Page,
Than all the double Meanings of the Stage.   20
    What needs he Paraphrase on what we mean?
We were at worst but Wanton; he's Obscene.
I, nor my Fellows, nor my Self excuse;
But Love's the Subject of the Comick Muse:
Nor can we write without it, nor would you   25
A Tale of only dry Instruction view;
Nor Love is always of a vicious Kind,
But oft to virtuous Acts inflames the Mind.
Awakes the sleepy Vigour of the Soul,

And, brushing o'er, adds Motion to the Pool.   30
Love, studious how to please, improves our Parts,
With polish'd Manners, and adorns with Arts.
Love first invented Verse, and form'd the Rhime,
The Motion measur'd, harmoniz'd the Chime;
To lib'ral Acts inlarg'd the narrow-Soul'd: 35
Soften'd the Fierce, and made the Coward Bold:
The World when wast, he Peopled with increase,
And warring Nations reconcil'd in Peace.
Ormond, the first, and all the Fair may find
In this one Legend to their Fame design'd,   }40
When Beauty fires the Blood, how Love exalts the Mind.

IN that sweet Isle, where *Venus* keeps her Court,
And ev'ry Grace, and all the Loves resort;
Where either Sex is form'd of softer Earth,
And takes the bent of Pleasure from their Birth;   45
There liv'd a *Cyprian* Lord, above the rest,
Wise, Wealthy, with a num'rous Issue blest.
   But as no Gift of Fortune is sincere,
Was only wanting in a worthy Heir:
His eldest Born a goodly Youth to view   50
Excell'd the rest in Shape, and outward Shew;
Fair, Tall, his Limbs with due Proportion join'd,
But of a heavy, dull, degenerate Mind.
His Soul bely'd the Features of his Face;
Beauty was there, but Beauty in disgrace.   55
A clownish Mien, a Voice with rustick sound,
And stupid Eyes, that ever lov'd the Ground.
He look'd like Nature's Error; as the Mind
And Body were not of a Piece design'd,   }
But made for two, and by mistake in one were join'd.   60
   The ruling Rod, the Father's forming Care,

Were exercis'd in vain, on Wit's despair;
The more inform'd the less he understood,
And deeper sunk by flound'ring in the Mud.
Now scorn'd of all, and grown the publick Shame,   65
The People from *Galesus* chang'd his Name,
And *Cymon* call'd, which signifies a Brute;
So well his Name did with his Nature sute.

    His Father, when he found his Labour lost,
And Care employ'd, that answer'd not the Cost,   70
Chose an ungrateful Object to remove,
And loath'd to see what Nature made him love;
So to his Country-Farm the Fool confin'd:
Rude Work well suted with a rustick Mind.
Thus to the Wilds the sturdy *Cymon* went,   75
A Squire among the Swains, and pleas'd with Banishment.
His Corn, and Cattle, were his only Care,
And his supreme Delight a Country-Fair.

  It happen'd on a Summers Holiday,
That to the Greenwood-shade he took his way;   } 80
For *Cymon* shun'd the Church, and us'd not much to Pray.
His Quarter-Staff, which he cou'd ne'er forsake,
Hung half before, and half behind his Back.
He trudg'd along unknowing what he sought,
And whistled as he went, for want of Thought.   85

  By Chance conducted, or by Thirst constrain'd,
The deep Recesses of the Grove he gain'd;
Where in a Plain, defended by the Wood,
Crept through the matted Grass a Chrystal Flood,   }
By which an Alablaster Fountain stood: 90
And on the Margin of the Fount was laid
(Attended by her Slaves) a sleeping Maid.
Like *Dian*, and her Nymphs, when tir'd with Sport,
To rest by cool *Eurotas* they resort:

The Dame herself the Goddess well express'd,   95
Not more distinguish'd by her Purple Vest,
Than by the charming Features of her Face,
And ev'n in Slumber a superiour Grace:
Her comely Limbs compos'd with decent Care, ⎫
Her Body shaded with a slight Cymarr;   ⎬   100
Her Bosom to the view was only bare: ⎭
Where two beginning Paps were scarcely spy'd,
For yet their Places were but signify'd:
The fanning Wind upon her Bosom blows,   ⎫
To meet the fanning Wind the Bosom rose;   ⎬   105
The fanning Wind, and purling Streams continue her ⎪
      repose.   ⎭

  The Fool of Nature, stood with stupid Eyes
And gaping Mouth, that testify'd Surprize,
Fix'd on her Face, nor cou'd remove his Sight,
New as he was to Love, and Novice in Delight: 110
Long mute he stood, and leaning on his Staff,
His Wonder witness'd with an Ideot laugh;
Then would have spoke, but by his glimmering Sense
First found his want of Words, and fear'd Offence:
Doubted for what he was he should be known,   115
By his Clown-Accent, and his Country-Tone.

  Through the rude Chaos thus the running Light
Shot the first Ray that pierc'd the Native Night:
Then Day and Darkness in the Mass were mix'd,
Till gather'd in a Globe, the Beams were fix'd: 120
Last shon the Sun who radiant in his Sphere
Illumin'd Heav'n, and Earth, and rowl'd around the Year.
So Reason in this Brutal Soul began:
Love made him first suspect he was a Man;
Love made him doubt his broad barbarian Sound,   125
By Love his want of Words, and Wit he found:

That sense of want prepar'd the future way
To Knowledge, and disclos'd the promise of a Day.
    What not his Father's Care, nor Tutor's Art
Cou'd plant with Pains in his unpolish'd Heart,   130
The best Instructor Love at once inspir'd,
As barren Grounds to Fruitfulness are fir'd:
Love taught him Shame, and Shame with Love at Strife
Soon taught the sweet Civilities of Life;
His gross material Soul at once could find   135
Somewhat in her excelling all her Kind:
Exciting a Desire till then unknown,
Somewhat unfound, or found in her alone.
This made the first Impression in his Mind,
Above, but just above the Brutal Kind.   140
For Beasts can like, but not distinguish too,
Nor their own liking by reflection know;
Nor why they like or this, or t'other Face,
Or judge of this or that peculiar Grace,
But love in gross, and stupidly admire;   145
As Flies allur'd by Light, approach the Fire.
Thus our Man-Beast advancing by degrees
First likes the whole, then sep'rates what he sees;
On sev'ral Parts a sev'ral Praise bestows,
The ruby Lips, the well-proportion'd Nose,   150
The snowy Skin, the Raven-glossy Hair,   ⎫
The dimpled Cheek, the Forehead rising fair,   ⎬
And ev'n in Sleep it self a smiling Air.   ⎭
From thence his Eyes descending view'd the rest,
Her plump round Arms, white Hands, and heaving Breast. 155
Long on the last he dwelt, though ev'ry part
A pointed Arrow sped to pierce his Heart.
    Thus in a trice a Judge of Beauty grown,
(A Judge erected from a Country-Clown)

He long'd to see her Eyes in Slumber hid;   160
And wish'd his own cou'd pierce within the Lid:
He wou'd have wak'd her, but restrain'd his Thought,
And Love new-born the first good Manners taught.
An awful Fear his ardent Wish withstood,
Nor durst disturb the Goddess of the Wood;   165
For such she seem'd by her celestial Face,
Excelling all the rest of human Race:
And Things divine by common Sense he knew,
Must be devoutly seen at distant view:
So checking his Desire, with trembling Heart   170
Gazing he stood, nor would, nor could depart;
Fix'd as a Pilgrim wilder'd in his way, ⎫
Who dares not stir by Night for fear to stray, ⎬
But stands with awful Eyes to watch the dawn of Day. ⎭

  At length awaking, *Iphigene* the Fair   175
(So was the Beauty call'd who caus'd his Care)
Unclos'd her Eyes, and double Day reveal'd,
While those of all her Slaves in Sleep were seal'd.

  The slavering Cudden prop'd upon his Staff,
Stood ready gaping with a grinning Laugh,   180
To welcome her awake, nor durst begin
To speak, but wisely kept the Fool within.
Then she; What make you *Cymon* here alone?
(For *Cymon*'s Name was round the Country known
Because descended of a noble Race,   185
And for a Soul ill sorted with his Face.)

  But still the Sot stood silent with Surprize,
With fix'd regard on her new open'd Eyes,
And in his Breast receiv'd th' invenom'd Dart,
A tickling Pain that pleas'd amid the Smart.   190
But conscious of her Form, with quick distrust
She saw his sparkling Eyes, and fear'd his brutal Lust:

This to prevent she wak'd her sleepy Crew,
And rising hasty took a short Adieu.

    Then *Cymon* first his rustick Voice essay'd,   195
With proffer'd Service to the parting Maid
To see her safe; his Hand she long deny'd,
But took at length, asham'd of such a Guide.
So *Cymon* led her home, and leaving there
No more wou'd to his Country Clowns repair,   200
But sought his Father's House with better Mind,
Refusing in the Farm to be confin'd.

    The Father wonder'd at the Son's return,
And knew not whether to rejoice or mourn;
But doubtfully receiv'd, expecting still   205
To learn the secret Causes of his alter'd Will.
Nor was he long delay'd; the first Request
He made, was, like his Brothers to be dress'd,
And, as his Birth requir'd, above the rest.

    With ease his Sute was granted by his Syre,   210
Distinguishing his Heir by rich Attire:
His Body thus adorn'd, he next design'd
With lib'ral Arts to cultivate his Mind:
He sought a Tutor of his own accord,
And study'd Lessons he before abhorr'd.   215

    Thus the Man-Child advanc'd, and learn'd so fast,
That in short time his Equals he surpass'd:
His brutal Manners from his Breast exil'd,
His Mien he fashion'd, and his Tongue he fil'd;
In ev'ry Exercise of all admir'd,   220
He seem'd, nor only seem'd, but was inspir'd:
Inspir'd by Love, whose Business is to please;
He Rode, he Fenc'd, he mov'd with graceful Ease,
More fam'd for Sense, for courtly Carriage more,
Than for his brutal Folly known before.   225

What then of alter'd *Cymon* shall we say,
But that the Fire which choak'd in Ashes lay,
A Load too heavy for his Soul to move,
Was upward blown below, and brush'd away by Love?
Love made an active Progress through his Mind,   230
The dusky Parts he clear'd, the gross refin'd;
The drowsy wak'd; and as he went impress'd
The Maker's Image on the human Beast.
Thus was the Man amended by Desire,
And tho' he lov'd perhaps with too much Fire,   235
His Father all his Faults with Reason scan'd,
And lik'd an error of the better Hand;
Excus'd th' excess of Passion in his Mind,
By Flames too fierce, perhaps too much refin'd:
So *Cymon*, since his Sire indulg'd his Will,   240
Impetuous lov'd, and would be *Cymon* still;
Galesus he disown'd, and chose to bear
The Name of Fool confirm'd, and Bishop'd by the Fair.
    To *Cipseus* by his Friends his Sute he mov'd,
Cipseus the Father of the Fair he lov'd: 245
But he was pre-ingag'd by former Ties,
While *Cymon* was endeav'ring to be wise:
And *Iphigene* oblig'd by former Vows,
Had giv'n her Faith to wed a Foreign Spouse:
Her Sire and She to *Rhodian Pasimond*,   250
Tho' both repenting, were by Promise bound,
Nor could retract; and thus, as Fate decreed,
Tho' better lov'd, he spoke too late to speed.
    The Doom was past, the Ship already sent,
Did all his tardy Diligence prevent: 255
Sigh'd to herself the fair unhappy Maid,
While stormy *Cymon* thus in secret said:
The time is come for *Iphigene* to find

The Miracle she wrought upon my Mind:
Her Charms have made me Man, her ravish'd Love   260
In rank shall place me with the Bless'd above.
For mine by Love, by Force she shall be mine,
Or Death, if Force should fail, shall finish my Design.
   Resolv'd he said: And rigg'd with speedy Care
A Vessel strong, and well equipp'd for War.   265
The secret Ship with chosen Friends he stor'd;
And bent to die, or conquer, went aboard.
Ambush'd he lay behind the *Cyprian* Shore,
Waiting the Sail that all his Wishes bore;
Nor long expected, for the following Tide   270
Sent out the hostile Ship and beauteous Bride.
   To *Rhodes* the Rival Bark directly steer'd,
When *Cymon* sudden at her Back appear'd,
And stop'd her Flight: Then standing on his Prow
In haughty Terms he thus defy'd the Foe,   275
Or strike your Sails at Summons, or prepare
To prove the last Extremities of War.
Thus warn'd, the *Rhodians* for the Fight provide;
Already were the Vessels Side by Side,
These obstinate to save, and those to seize the Bride.   280
But *Cymon* soon his crooked Grapples cast,
Which with tenacious hold his Foes embrac'd,
And arm'd with Sword and Shield, amid the Press he pass'd.
Fierce was the Fight, but hast'ning to his Prey,
By force the furious Lover freed his way: 285
Himself alone dispers'd the *Rhodian* Crew,
The Weak disdain'd, the Valiant overthrew;
Cheap Conquest for his following Friends remain'd,
He reap'd the Field, and they but only glean'd.
   His Victory confess'd, the Foes retreat,   290
And cast their Weapons at the Victor's Feet.

Whom thus he chear'd: O *Rhodian* Youth, I fought
For Love alone, nor other Booty sought;
Your Lives are safe; your Vessel I resign,
Yours be your own, restoring what is mine: 295
In *Iphigene* I claim my rightful Due,
Rob'd by my Rival, and detain'd by you:
Your *Pasimond* a lawless Bargain drove,
The Parent could not sell the Daughters Love;
Or if he cou'd, my Love disdains the Laws,   300
And like a King by Conquest gains his Cause:
Where Arms take place, all other Pleas are vain,
Love taught me Force, and Force shall Love maintain.
You, what by Strength you could not keep, release,
And at an easy Ransom buy your Peace.   305
   Fear on the conquer'd Side soon sign'd th' Accord,
And *Iphigene* to *Cymon* was restor'd:
While to his Arms the blushing Bride he took,
To seeming Sadness she compos'd her Look;
As if by Force subjected to his Will,   310
Tho' pleas'd, dissembling, and a Woman still.
And, for she wept, he wip'd her falling Tears,
And pray'd her to dismiss her empty Fears;
For yours I am, he said, and have deserv'd
Your Love much better whom so long I serv'd,   315
Than he to whom your formal Father ty'd
Your Vows; and sold a Slave, not sent a Bride.
Thus while he spoke he seiz'd the willing Prey,
As *Paris* bore the *Spartan* Spouse away:
Faintly she scream'd, and ev'n her Eyes confess'd   320
She rather would be thought, than was Distress'd.
   Who now exults but *Cymon* in his Mind, ⎫
Vain hopes, and empty Joys of human Kind, ⎬
Proud of the present, to the future blind! ⎭

Secure of Fate while *Cymon* plows the Sea,   325
And steers to *Candy* with his conquer'd Prey,
Scarce the third Glass of measur'd Hours was run,
When like a fiery Meteor sunk the Sun;
The Promise of a Storm; the shifting Gales
Forsake by Fits, and fill the flagging Sails: 330
Hoarse Murmurs of the Main from far were heard,
And Night came on, not by degrees prepar'd,
But all at once; at once the Winds arise,
The Thunders roul, the forky Lightning flies:
In vain the Master issues out Commands,   335
In vain the trembling Sailors ply their Hands:
The Tempest unforeseen prevents their Care,
And from the first they labour in despair.
The giddy Ship betwixt the Winds and Tides
Forc'd back and forwards, in a Circle rides,   340
Stun'd with the diff'rent Blows; then shoots amain
Till counterbuff'd she stops, and sleeps again.
Not more aghast the proud Archangel fell,
Plung'd from the height of Heav'n to deepest Hell,
Than stood the Lover of his Love possess'd,   345
Now curs'd the more, the more he had been bless'd;
More anxious for her Danger than his own,
Death he defies; but would be lost alone.
   Sad *Iphigene* to Womanish Complaints
Adds pious Pray'rs, and wearies all the Saints;   350
Ev'n if she could, her Love she would repent,
But since she cannot, dreads the Punishment:
Her forfeit Faith, and *Pasimond* betray'd,
Are ever present, and her Crime upbraid.
She blames herself, nor blames her Lover less,   355
Augments her Anger as her Fears increase;
From her own Back the Burden would remove,

And lays the Load on his ungovern'd Love,
Which interposing durst in Heav'n's despight
Invade, and violate another's Right: 360
The Pow'rs incens'd awhile deferr'd his Pain,
And made him Master of his Vows in vain:
But soon they punish'd his presumptuous Pride;⎞
That for his daring Enterprize she dy'd,   ⎬
Who rather not resisted, than comply'd.   ⎠   365

  Then impotent of Mind, with alter'd Sense,
She hugg'd th' Offender, and forgave th' Offence,
Sex to the last: Mean time with Sails declin'd
The wand'ring Vessel drove before the Wind:
Toss'd, and retoss'd, aloft, and then alow;   ⎞   370
Nor Port they seek, nor certain Course they know, ⎬
Bur ev'ry moment wait the coming Blow.   ⎠
Thus blindly driv'n, by breaking Day they view'd
The Land before 'em, and their Fears renew'd;
The Land was welcome, but the Tempest bore   375
The threaten'd Ship against a rocky Shore.

  A winding Bay was near; to this they bent,
And just escap'd; their Force already spent:
Secure from Storms and panting from the Sea,
The Land unknown at leisure they survey;   380
And saw (but soon their sickly Sight withdrew)
The rising Tow'rs of *Rhodes* at distant view;
And curs'd the hostile Shoar of *Pasimond*,
Sav'd from the Seas, and shipwreck'd on the Ground.

  The frighted Sailors try'd their Strength in vain   385
To turn the Stern, and tempt the stormy Main;
But the stiff Wind withstood the lab'ring Oar,
And forc'd them forward on the fatal Shoar!
The crooked Keel now bites the *Rhodian* Strand,
And the Ship moor'd, constrains the Crew to land: 390

Yet still they might be safe because unknown,
But as ill Fortune seldom comes alone,
The Vessel they dismiss'd was driv'n before,
Already shelter'd on their Native Shoar;
Known each, they know: But each with change of
    Chear;   395
The vanquish'd side exults; the Victors fear,
Not them but theirs; made Pris'ners e'er they Fight,
Despairing Conquest, and depriv'd of Flight.
   The Country rings around with loud Alarms,
And raw in Fields the rude Militia swarms;   400
Mouths without Hands; maintain'd at vast Expence,
In Peace a Charge, in War a weak Defence:
Stout once a Month they march a blust'ring Band,
And ever, but in times of Need, at hand:
This was the Morn when issuing on the Guard,   405
Drawn up in Rank and File they stood prepar'd
Of seeming Arms to make a short essay,
Then hasten to be Drunk, the Business of the Day.
   The Cowards would have fled, but that they knew
Themselves so many, and their Foes so few;   410
But crowding on, the last the first impel;
Till overborn with weight the *Cyprians* fell.
Cymon inslav'd, who first the War begun,
And *Iphigene* once more is lost and won.
   Deep in a Dungeon was the Captive cast,   415
Depriv'd of Day, and held in Fetters fast:
His Life was only spar'd at their Request,
Whom taken he so nobly had releas'd:
But *Iphigenia* was the Ladies Care,
Each in their turn address'd to treat the Fair;   420
While *Pasimond* and his, the Nuptial Feast pre-
    pare.

Her secret Soul to *Cymon* was inclin'd,
But she must suffer what her Fates assign'd;
So passive is the Church of Womankind.
What worse to *Cymon* could his Fortune deal,   425
Rowl'd to the lowest Spoke of all her Wheel?
It rested to dismiss the downward weight,
Or raise him upward to his former height;
The latter pleas'd; and Love (concern'd the most)
Prepar'd th' amends, for what by Love he lost.   430

The Sire of *Pasimond* had left a Son,
Though younger, yet for Courage early known,
Ormisda call'd; to whom by Promise ty'd,
A *Rhodian* Beauty was the destin'd Bride:
Cassandra was her Name, above the rest   435
Renown'd for Birth, with Fortune amply bless'd.
Lysymachus who rul'd the *Rhodian* State,
Was then by choice their annual Magistrate:
He lov'd *Cassandra* too with equal Fire,
But Fortune had not favour'd his Desire;   440
Cross'd by her Friends, by her not disapprov'd,
Nor yet preferr'd, or like *Ormisda* lov'd:
So stood th' Affair: Some little Hope remain'd,
That should his Rival chance to lose, he gain'd.

Mean time young *Pasimond* his Marriage press'd,   445
Ordain'd the Nuptial Day, prepar'd the Feast;
And frugally resolv'd (the Charge to shun,
Which would be double should he wed alone)
To join his Brother's Bridal with his own.

Lysymachus oppress'd with mortal Grief   450
Receiv'd the News, and study'd quick Relief:
The fatal Day approach'd: If Force were us'd,
The Magistrate his publick Trust abus'd;
To Justice, liable as Law requir'd;

For when his Office ceas'd, his Pow'r expir'd: 455
While Pow'r remain'd, the Means were in his Hand
By Force to seize, and then forsake the Land:
Betwixt Extreams he knew not how to move,
A Slave to Fame, but more a Slave to Love:
Restraining others, yet himself not free,   460
Made impotent by Pow'r, debas'd by Dignity!
Both Sides he weigh'd: But after much Debate,
The Man prevail'd above the Magistrate.

   Love never fails to master what he finds,
But works a diff'rent way in diff'rent Minds,   465
The Fool enlightens, and the Wise he blinds.
This Youth proposing to possess, and scape,
Began in Murder, to conclude in Rape:
Unprais'd by me, tho' Heav'n sometime may bless
An impious Act with undeserv'd Success: 470
The Great, it seems, are priviledg'd alone
To punish all Injustice but their own.
But here I stop, not daring to proceed,
Yet blush to flatter an unrighteous Deed:
For Crimes are but permitted, not decreed.   475

   Resolv'd on Force, his Wit the Pretor bent,
To find the Means that might secure th' event;
Not long he labour'd, for his lucky Thought
In Captive *Cymon* found the Friend he sought;
Th' Example pleas'd: The Cause and Crime the same;   480
An injur'd Lover, and a ravish'd Dame.
How much he durst he knew by what he dar'd,
The less he had to lose, the less he car'd
To menage loathsom Life when Love was the Re-
    ward.

   This ponder'd well, and fix'd on his Intent,   485
In depth of Night he for the Pris'ner sent;

In secret sent, the publick View to shun,
Then with a sober Smile he thus begun.
The Pow'rs above who bounteously bestow
Their Gifts and Graces on Mankind below,   490
Yet prove our Merit first, nor blindly give
To such as are not worthy to receive:
For Valour and for Virtue they provide
Their due Reward, but first they must be try'd:
These fruitful Seeds within your Mind they sow'd;   495
'Twas yours t' improve the Talent they bestow'd:
They gave you to be born of noble Kind,
They gave you Love to lighten up your Mind,
And purge the grosser Parts; they gave you Care
To please, and Courage to deserve the Fair.   500
   Thus far they try'd you, and by Proof they found
The Grain intrusted in a grateful Ground:
But still the great Experiment remain'd,
They suffer'd you to lose the Prize you gain'd;
That you might learn the Gift was theirs alone: 505
And when restor'd, to them the Blessing own.
Restor'd it soon will be; the Means prepar'd,
The Difficulty smooth'd, the Danger shar'd:
Be but your self, the Care to me resign,
Then *Iphigene* is yours, *Cassandra* mine.   510
Your Rival *Pasimond* pursues your Life,
Impatient to revenge his ravish'd Wife,
But yet not his; to Morrow is behind,
And Love our Fortunes in one Band has join'd:
Two Brothers are our Foes; *Ormisda* mine,   515
As much declar'd, as *Pasimond* is thine:
To Morrow must their common Vows be ty'd; }
With Love to Friend and Fortune for our Guide, }
Let both resolve to die, or each redeem a Bride. }

Right I have none, nor hast thou much to plead;   520
'Tis Force when done must justify the Deed:
Our Task perform'd we next prepare for Flight;
And let the Losers talk in vain of Right:
We with the Fair will sail before the Wind,
If they are griev'd, I leave the Laws behind.   525
Speak thy Resolves; if now thy Courage droop,
Despair in Prison, and abandon Hope;
But if thou dar'st in Arms thy Love regain,
(For Liberty without thy Love were vain:)
Then second my Design to seize the Prey,   530
Or lead to second Rape, for well thou know'st the way.
    Said *Cymon* overjoy'd, do Thou propose
The Means to Fight, and only shew the Foes;
For from the first, when Love had fir'd my Mind,
Resolv'd I left the Care of Life behind.   535
    To this the bold *Lysymachus* reply'd,
Let Heav'n be neuter, and the Sword decide:
The Spousals are prepar'd, already play
The Minstrels, and provoke the tardy Day:
By this the Brides are wak'd, their Grooms are dress'd;⎫   540
All *Rhodes* is summon'd to the Nuptial Feast,   ⎬
All but my self the sole unbidden Guest.   ⎭
Unbidden though I am, I will be there,
And, join'd by thee, intend to joy the Fair.
    Now hear the rest; when Day resigns the Light,   545
And chearful Torches guild the jolly Night;
Be ready at my Call, my chosen few
With Arms administer'd shall aid thy Crew.
Then entring unexpected will we seize
Our destin'd Prey, from Men dissolv'd in ease;   550
By Wine disabled, unprepar'd for Fight;
And hast'ning to the Seas suborn our Flight:

The Seas are ours, for I command the Fort,
A Ship well man'd, expects us in the Port:
If they, or if their Friends the Prize contest,   555
Death shall attend the Man who dares resist.

  It pleas'd! The Pris'ner to his Hold retir'd,
His Troop with equal Emulation fir'd,
All fix'd to Fight, and all their wonted Work requir'd.

  The Sun arose; the Streets were throng'd around,   560
The Palace open'd, and the Posts were crown'd:
The double Bridegroom at the Door attends
Th' expected Spouse, and entertains the Friends:
They meet, they lead to Church; the Priests invoke
The Pow'rs, and feed the Flames with fragrant Smoke: 565
This done they Feast, and at the close of Night
By kindled Torches vary their Delight,
These lead the lively Dance, and those the brimming Bowls
    invite.

  Now at th' appointed Place and Hour assign'd,
With Souls resolv'd the Ravishers were join'd: 570
Three Bands are form'd: The first is sent before
To favour the Retreat, and guard the Shore:
The second at the Palace-gate is plac'd,
And up the lofty Stairs ascend the last:
A peaceful Troop they seem with shining Vests,   575
But Coats of Male beneath secure their Breasts.

  Dauntless they enter, *Cymon* at their Head,
And find the Feast renew'd, the Table spread:
Sweet Voices mix'd with instrumental Sounds
Ascend the vaulted Roof, the vaulted Roof rebounds.   580
When like the Harpies rushing through the Hall
The suddain Troop appears, the Tables fall,
Their smoaking Load is on the Pavement thrown;
Each Ravisher prepares to seize his own:

The Brides invaded with a rude Embrace 585
Shreek out for Aid, Confusion fills the Place:
Quick to redeem the Prey their plighted Lords
Advance, the Palace gleams with shining Swords.
  But late is all Defence, and Succour vain;
The Rape is made, the Ravishers remain: 590
Two sturdy Slaves were only sent before
To bear the purchas'd Prize in Safety to the Shore.
The Troop retires, the Lovers close the rear,
With forward Faces not confessing Fear:
Backward they move, but scorn their Pace to mend, 595
Then seek the Stairs, and with slow hast descend.
  Fierce *Pasimond* their passage to prevent,
Thrust full on *Cymon*'s Back in his descent,
The Blade return'd unbath'd, and to the Handle bent:
Stout *Cymon* soon remounts, and cleft in two 600
His Rival's Head with one descending Blow:
And as the next in rank *Ormisda* stood,
He turn'd the Point: The Sword inur'd to Blood,
Bor'd his unguarded Breast, which pour'd a purple
    Flood.
  With vow'd Revenge the gath'ring Crowd pursues, 605
The Ravishers turn Head, the Fight renews;
The Hall is heap'd with Corps; the sprinkled Gore
Besmears the Walls, and floats the Marble Floor.
Dispers'd at length the drunken Squadron flies,
The Victors to their Vessel bear the Prize; 610
And hear behind loud Groans, and lamentable Cries.
  The Crew with merry Shouts their Anchors weigh
Then ply their Oars, and brush the buxom Sea,
While Troops of gather'd *Rhodians* croud the Key.
What should the People do, when left alone? 615
The Governor, and Government are gone.

The publick Wealth to Foreign Parts convey'd;
Some Troops disbanded, and the rest unpaid.
Rhodes is the Soveraign of the Sea no more;
Their Ships unrigg'd, and spent their Naval Store;   620
They neither could defend, nor can pursue,
But grind their Teeth, and cast a helpless view:
In vain with Darts a distant War they try,
Short, and more short the missive Weapons fly.
Mean while the Ravishers their Crimes enjoy,   625
And flying Sails, and sweeping Oars employ;
The Cliffs of *Rhodes* in little space are lost,
Jove's Isle they seek; nor *Jove* denies his Coast.
  In safety landed on the *Candian* Shore,
With generous Wines their Spirits they restore;   630
There *Cymon* with his *Rhodian* Friend resides,
Both Court, and Wed at once the willing Brides.
A War ensues, the *Cretans* own their Cause,
Stiff to defend their hospitable Laws:
Both Parties lose by turns; and neither wins,   635
'Till Peace propounded by a Truce begins.
The Kindred of the Slain forgive the Deed,
But a short Exile must for Show precede;
The Term expir'd, from *Candia* they remove;
And happy each at Home, enjoys his Love.   640

NOTES

PAGE 37. PROLOGUE TO THE ASSIGNATION. Dryden's comedy was first performed by the King's company at the old Duke's theatre in Lincoln's Inn Fields in October 1672.

13. *split*: suffer shipwreck.

20. *what Farces hit*. The rise of stage farce in the 1670's caused concern among serious dramatists, and is a common theme for satire. Cf. Epilogue to *The Wild Gallant Reviv'd*, ll. 41–48.

24. *Th' unnatural strain'd Buffoon*: the gross and crudely drawn character of farce, often in the old tradition of 'humours' comedy.

27. *lin'd*: draped, covered.

29. *oyl'd Coates*, of cloth impregnated and waterproofed with oil, became common about this time.

30. *Mamamouchi*: the pseudo-Turkish title said to have been conferred by the sultan on M. Jourdain in Molière's *Le Bourgeois gentilhomme*, IV. iii. Dryden refers specifically to Edward Ravenscroft's *The Citizen turn'd Gentleman*, performed three months earlier at Dorset Garden with outrageous success.

34–37. *Sure . . . Mamamouchi*. In Ravenscroft's play, V, Jorden is invested as a Mamamouchi or Paladin to the accompaniment of 'Hula baba la chou' and other gibberish. 'I am beholden to you', he exclaims in Act IV, 'for telling me, for I could ne'er have thought that *Marababa sahem*, should signifie, Ah how much in love am I! Ah this Turkish is a most admirable language.'

38. *Grimace and habit*: affected, exaggerated acting and stage costume.

40. *had*: would have.

45. The speaker of the Prologue is Joseph Haines (1648–1701), at one time a Latin secretary; a skilful dancer and comedian, celebrated for his speaking of prologues and epilogues rather than for acting.

PAGE 38. EPILOGUE TO THE WILD GALLANT REVIV'D. First performed at the Theatre Royal in Vere Street in February 1663, this comedy was, says Dryden, 'more than once the Divertisement of His Majesty, by His own Command . . . the first attempt I made in *Dramatick Poetry*.'

3. *in level*: accessible, intelligible.

11–12. *like Turkes . . . meat.* Turkish soldiers 'never drinke any thing but water, and feed on nothing but rice, and drie-salt flesh, which they reduce into a kinde of powder . . . and for a shift, will live a long time with the bloud of their horses' (Montaigne, *Essais*, 1. xlviii; transl. Florio). *Treat*: feast. *Regallio's*: choice fare.

17. *Prizes*: wrestling-matches or contests with weapons. Cf. Pepys, *Diary*, 1 June 1663, 12 April 1669.

22. *Press*: warrant authorizing compulsory enlistment for service in the navy.

24. *charge an Oph upon*: demand the contribution of one idiot (oaf) from.

25. *Traind-Bands*: trained companies of citizen militia, which Dryden ridiculed more than once. Cf. *Cymon and Iphigenia*, ll. 399–412.

34: *tawdry*: 'tricked up with such tinsel Stuff, or Lace, as is usually sold at Audery-Fair in Cambridge-shire' (Phillips, *New World of Words*, 1706 edn.).

36. *take*: hold the attention of, win favour with.

38. *writ of ease*: certificate of discharge from employment.

39. *Land-tax*: assessed on landed property. The old 'subsidy' on land was revived in 1663; and a land tax was imposed in 1677.

41–44. *Would you . . . become.* Cf. Prologue to *The Assignation*, ll. 20 ff.

44. *Vests*: Charles II's 'own Fashion', a knee-length vest and surcoat, assumed in October 1666; recommended by John Evelyn in imitation of Persian costume. See his *Diary*, 18 October 1666. 'A general Humour, in opposition to *France*, had made us throw off their Fashion, and put on Vests, that we might look more like a distinct People, and not be under the servility of imitation' (Halifax, *Works*, ed. Raleigh, p. 90).

48. *staple Trade*: the market in goods which are their monopoly.

PAGE 40. PROLOGUE TO THE SECOND PART OF THE CONQUEST OF GRANADA. On 9 February 1671 Evelyn records a performance, at Whitehall, of this 'famous Play . . . two days acted successively' with 'very glorious scenes and perspectives' by the king's serjeant-painter. The Prologue to the Second Part was spoken by the celebrated actor Michael Mohun (d. 1684).

10. *Scriv'ners*: here 'money scriveners', brokers who placed out clients' money at interest and made loans on security. A contemporary

manuscript of this prologue, possibly derived from the actors, gives four
additional lines after l. 10:

> Some of them seeme indeede ye Poetts freinds;
> But 'tis, as France courts England, for her ends.
> They build up this Lampoone, & th' other Songe,
> And Court him, to lye still, while they grow stronge.

Dryden had detractors at court at this time; and these lines may refer
to the Duke of Buckingham and his friends, who had been preparing
a dramatic skit on Dryden in *The Rehearsal* (performed 7 December
1671).

13. *Vizard Masque*: a whore. The mask worn by ladies of fashion after
the Restoration (cf. Pepys, *Diary*, 12 June 1663) soon became a trade-
mark of prostitution (ibid. 18 February 1667). In Dryden's *Kind Keeper*
(1680), IV. i, two squabbling whores are pacified with 'At the Play-
houses, she shall ply the Boxes, because she has the better Face; and
you shall have the Pit, because you can prattle best out of a *Vizor-Mask*'.

15–16. *Perks up . . . Face*. Combing the wig in public was a foppish
habit. Cf. a prologue printed in *Covent Garden Drollery* (1672, p. 33):

> He who comes hither with design to hiss,
> And with a bum revers'd, to whisper Miss,
> To comb a Perriwig, or to shew gay cloathes,
> Or to vent Antique nonsense with new oathes,
> Our Poet welcomes . . . .

The white wig did not supplant the periwig until the first decade of
the eighteenth century; but it became a mark of fashion in the 1670's.

19–20. *the whole noise of Fopps . . . no*. For an account of playhouse
manners see A. Nicoll, *A History of . . . Restoration Drama*, 1952,
pp. 15–19.

PAGE 41. PROLOGUE TO THE UNIVERSITY OF OXFORD. One of the
pieces written for presentation during the Oxford 'Acts' which, as
there was no professional theatre, were given mainly in the tennis-
courts. This poem, though not published until 1684, is transcribed in
a manuscript collection of 1676. Sending Rochester copies of a prologue
and epilogue 'made for our players when they went down to Oxford'
in 1673, Dryden says: 'I heare since, they have succeeded; And by the
event your Lordship will judge how easy 'tis to passe any thing upon
an University; and how grosse flattery the learned will endure.' The

opposition of London and Oxford audiences in ll. 11–24 is a common-place; the extremity of adulation is reached in ll. 35–38.

5–6. *Trade in Ore . . . Shore*. Cf. the Spaniard Vasquez in Mexico, in Dryden's *The Indian Emperour* (1667), I. i: 'Methinks we walk in Dreams on Fairy Land, / Where Golden Ore lies mixt with common Sand.'

31–32. *Not . . . Provincial Band*. For a provincial community the first step towards Roman citizenship was the receipt of the *ius Latii*, which did not include the privilege of the *ius suffragii*. The poets, says Dryden, ask not for full membership of the University but merely for the advantages of association.

PAGE 42. PROLOGUE TO THE DUTCHESS ON HER RETURN FROM SCOTLAND. As opposition to the papist Duke of York hardened into Whig demands that he should be excluded from the succession, Charles II kept him out of the country as much as possible: he spent the winter of 1679–80 and October 1680–March 1682 in Scotland, and returned to Edinburgh in May 1682 to bring his wife home. They reached White-hall amid 'publick expressions of joy' on 27 May. Dryden's prologue, one of many poems to mark the occasion, was written for a special performance of Otway's *Venice Preserv'd* and separately published. Five years earlier he had paid tribute to the duchess's beauty in the Dedication of *The State of Innocence*: 'You render Mankind insensible to other Beauties; and have destroy'd the Empire of Love, in a Court which was the Seat of his Dominion . . . and reign absolute over the Hearts of a stubborn and free-born People, tenacious almost to Madness of their Liberty.'

24–25. *Like Joseph's Dream . . . come*. Gen. xli.

PAGE 44. ABSALOM AND ACHITOPHEL. This poem deals with the political crisis of 1679–81, precipitated by Whig opposition to Charles II. The policy of the Whigs, led by the Earl of Shaftesbury, included anti-popery and the destruction of the alliance with Catholic France; and the party were set to exclude the papist Duke of York, Charles II's brother and heir, and to promote the rival claim of the king's bastard son Monmouth as 'the great confessor for the protestant religion'. Suspicion of York was intensified in 1679, after Titus Oates had laid a narrative of Jesuit conspiracy before the king, and persuaded the Commons that there was 'a damnable and hellish plot, contrived and carried on by Popish recusants, for the assassinating and murdering

the king, and for subverting the government and destroying the Protestant religion'. After more than two years of crisis and of executions
for complicity in the Popish Plot, the tide began to turn for the king.
Oates and his fellows discredited themselves as witnesses. At Oxford,
in March 1681, Charles dissolved Parliament; and in April he made
a successful appeal to the country in *His Majesties Declaration To all his
Loving Subjects*. Early in July Shaftesbury was committed to the Tower
on a charge of high treason; and *Absalom and Achitophel*, said to have
been written at the king's request, was published in November probably with the design of prejudicing Shaftesbury's imminent trial. The
poem recounts the story of the exclusionist campaign, the Plot, and
Shaftesbury's seduction of Monmouth, with character-sketches of the
king's enemies and his friends, in an elaborate allegorical application
of the Biblical history of David, Absalom, and Achitophel. The portraits selected here are from ll. 150–219 and 543–681 of the poem.

1. *the false Achitophel*: Anthony Ashley Cooper (1621–83), who fought
on the royalist side in the Civil War; became one of Cromwell's
council; was associated with Charles II's return in 1660; and in 1672
was made Earl of Shaftesbury and Lord Chancellor, an office in which
he conducted himself with dignity and distinction (cf. ll. 38–42). Dis-
missed in 1673, he moved into opposition and became leader of the
'country' (Whig) party. 'He had', says Bishop Burnet, 'a wonderful
faculty in speaking to a popular assembly' and 'a particular talent to make
others trust to his judgment, and depend on it. . . . He had a wonderful faculty at opposing, and running things down. . . . He was not
ashamed to reckon up the many turns he had made: And he valued himself on the doing it at the properest season, and in the best manner.'

4. *wit*: imagination.

5. *Place*: office, position.

9. *o'r inform'd*: animated excessively.

14. *Wits*: geniuses. Cf. Seneca, *De Tranq. Animi*, xvii. 10, 'nullum
magnum ingenium sine mixtura dementiae fuit': 'there has been no
great genius without some mixture of madness.'

21–23. Dryden applies the supposedly Platonic definition of man,
'a two-legged unfeathered animal', to Shaftesbury's son Anthony, born
two weeks before his father, trying 'hudled Notions', joined a committee of Cromwell's Parliament in 1652.

26–28. *To Compass this . . . Yoke*. In 1668 England formed the Triple
Alliance with Holland and Sweden; but in May 1670 Charles signed

the secret Treaty of Dover with Louis XIV. In return for subsidies Charles was to declare himself a Roman Catholic at an opportune moment (which never came), and join with France against the Dutch. Shaftesbury shares responsibility for involving England in the war against Holland in 1672, but hardly for fitting her to the foreign yoke of France. Dryden, however, turns popular fear of France, and the suspicion that the war had been a camouflage for arbitrary designs and popery, to polemical account against him.

30. *a Patriott's All-attoning Name.* Cf. the anonymous *Character of a Disbanded Courtier* (1681): 'Having lost his Honour with his Prince, . . . he cringes, and creeps, and sneaks, to the lowest and basest of the People, to procure himself . . . an empty, vain-glorious, and undeserved Name, the *Patriot* of his Country.'

31–42. *So easie . . . Access.* These lines were added in the second edition. Lines 31–36 are a rhetorical elaboration of 29–30; 37–42 are an explanatory elaboration of 43–44, and enhance the effect of Dryden's satire by balancing blame with praise.

39. *Abbethdin*: 'father of the court of justice', one of the two presiding judges of the Jewish civil court.

44. *the Gown*: the profession of the law.

46. *Cockle*: weeds. Cf. Shakespeare, *Coriolanus*, III. i. 67–70: in soothing 'the mutable ranke sented Meynie' we nourish 'the Cockle of Rebellion, Insolence, Sedition'.

47–48. 'David would have sung his praises instead of writing a psalm, and so Heaven would have had one immortal song the less.'

51. *to possess*: of possessing.

55. *manifest of Crimes*: his crimes apparent. A latinism. Cf. Sallust, *Bellum Iugurthinum*, xxxv. 8, 'Iugurtha manifestus tanti sceleris'.

59. *The wish'd occasion . . . he takes.* The Whigs patronized and encouraged Oates. Shaftesbury is said to have remarked, on the Plot, 'I will not say who started the Game, but I am sure I had the full Hunting of it.' A certain lord, says Roger North, asked Shaftesbury 'what he intended to do with the Plot, which was so full of Nonsense. . . . Its no Matter, said he, the more Nonsensical the better; if we cannot bring them to swallow worse Nonsense than that, we shall never do any Good with them.'

64. *Jebusite*: Roman Catholic. Joshua xv. 63.

67–70. *Prime*: the beginning of a cycle; confusedly applied to the 'golden number', the number of any year in the lunar cycle of nineteen years. Dryden refers to English demands for a change of government at intervals of about nineteen years: the Long Parliament, the Restoration, and the troubles of 1679–81.

72. *Zimri*: George Villiers (1628–87), second Duke of Buckingham; between 1667 and 1674 Charles's chief minister, thereafter associated with the Whigs. Bishop Burnet's prose 'character' of Buckingham is a parallel to Dryden's verse: 'He had a great liveliness of wit, and a peculiar faculty of turning all things into ridicule: . . . he was drawn into chymistry: And for some years he thought he was very near the finding the philosopher's stone. . . . He had no principles of religion, vertue, or friendship. Pleasure, frolick, or extravagant diversion was all that he laid to heart. He was true to nothing, for he was not true to himself. He had no steadiness nor conduct. . . . He could never fix his thoughts, nor govern his estate, tho' then the greatest in *England*.' Dryden is probably recalling Zimri, servant of Elah and captain of half his chariots, who conspired against him (1 Kings xvi. 8–20; 2 Kings ix. 31).

99. *Common-wealthsmen*: republicans who hoped, by altering the succession, to recover the power they had enjoyed under Cromwell. Cf. *The Medall*, l. 216, note.

102. *well hung Balaam and cold Caleb*. Balaam is probably either (i) Theophilus Hastings (1650–1701), seventh Earl of Huntingdon, who repented of his adherence to Shaftesbury and was received back into royal favour in 1681 (cf. 2 Pet. ii. 15–16; Num. xxiii. 11); or (ii) Sir Francis Winnington (1634–1700), Charles's solicitor-general in 1674, but from 1678 a supporter of the Exclusion Bill, and 'a famous Pleader' (Evelyn). *Well hung*, a double entendre: fluent (cf. Num. xxii. 5–6), and licentious (Rev. ii. 14). Caleb is probably Arthur Capel (1632–83), Earl of Essex, viceroy in Ireland 1672–7, an exclusionist, and 'a sober, wise, judicious, and pondering person' (Evelyn).

103. *Canting Nadab*: William, Lord Howard of Escrick (1626–94), formerly a sectarian preacher. 'He was a man of a pleasant conversation,' says Burnet; 'but he railed so indecently both at the King and the Clergy, that I was very uneasy in his company.' *Porridge*: hotch-potch; applied by dissenters to the Anglican services and prayer-book. In March 1681 Edward Fitzharris, an Irish informer for the court, was charged with framing a libel on the king, and accused Howard of being the author. Howard was committed to the Tower, and is said there to have taken the Sacrament according to the Book of Common Prayer, using lamb's wool (a hot ale mixed with the pulp of roasted apples) for

wine. Howard's pseudonym is appropriate: Nadab was a son of Aaron the Levite (Exod. vi. 23; Dryden's name for dissenting ministers), and 'offered strange fire before the Lord, which he commanded them not' (Lev. x. 1).

109. *Jonas*: Sir William Jones (1631–82), attorney-general and director of prosecutions for the Plot until November 1679; thereafter an exclusionist.

113. *Shimei*: Slingsby Bethel (1617–97), elected one of London's two Whig sheriffs in 1680. He had been a republican from the first, and in 1660 was employed to raise troops against those who were restoring Charles II. 'He was', says Burnet, 'a sullen and wilful man; and turned from the ordinary way of a Sheriff's living into the extream of sordidness, which was very unacceptable to the body of the citizens, and proved a great prejudice to the party.' After his election, which was contrived by the Whigs, 'it was said, that the King would not have common justice done him hereafter against any of them, how guilty soever. The setting up *Bethel* gave a great colour to this jealousy; for it was said, he had expressed his approving the late King's death in very indecent terms.'

123. *Vare*: a staff carried as a symbol of office (Spanish *vara*).

126. *The Sons of Belial*: connotes drunkenness and immorality (Judges xix. 22–25; Milton, *Paradise Lost*, i. 500–5). But Dryden refers primarily to rebellion (cf. Deut. xiii. 13 and 2 Sam. xx. 1–2). The familiar pun on 'Balliol/Belial' was applied to the Whigs at the time of the Oxford Parliament (1681), when Balliol College accommodated the Whig leaders.

143. *Clog*: obstacle (lit. a block tied to a horse's leg to impede it).

145. *Rechabite*: see Jer. xxxv.

160. *Corah*: Titus Oates (1649–1705), son of a Norfolk weaver turned preacher; received into the Roman Church in 1677, expelled from the English College at Valladolid and returned with ignominy from the seminary at St. Omers in 1678. His experience of Catholic institutions was manipulated to fill out the fictitious narrative of the Plot. By mid-1681 his credit as saviour of the nation, and his terrible power as a witness, were in decline. Dryden's satire struck him at the crisis of his fortunes. Cf. Num. xvi.

161. *thou Monumental Brass*. Numbers xxi. 6–9. Dryden may also be recalling the Old Testament application of 'brass' to 'a people impudent in sin' (cf. Jer. vi. 28).

169. *Enobles all his Bloud.* Oates indeed, embarrassed by his mean birth, had his pedigree made out and his arms engraved on his table plate.

170-1. *Who ever . . . Stephen grace.* Acts vi. 9-15.

173. *His Tribe were Godalmightys Gentlemen.* See Num. xvi. 8-9.

175. *Sure signs . . . proud.* Ironic; Oates's conduct fits traditional accounts of choleric men, 'bold and impudent, . . . impatient in discourse, stiff, irrefragable and prodigious in their tenents; and if they be moved, most violent, outragious, ready to disgrace' (Burton, *Anatomy of Melancholy*, I. iii. I. 3).

177. *A Church Vermilion, and a Moses's Face.* Corah has the red face of the sensual priest of comedy; but Dryden ironically interprets his brightness as the illumination of the prophet, and compares the revealer of the Plot with Moses, whose face shone when he came down from Sinai with the tables of testimony (Exod. xxxiv. 29).

185-7. *The Spirit . . . University.* Oates claimed that while at Valladolid he travelled to Salamanca and was admitted Doctor of Divinity. The Salamanca authorities strenuously denied this.

196-9. *Were I . . . my Plot.* It had become apparent that personal malice underlay many of Oates's accusations.

200-1. *His Zeal . . . indignities.* Oates lived with insulting flamboyance at Whitehall, accused the queen of high treason, and charged her physician with complicity in a plot to poison Charles with her approval.

204-5. *Agag*: probably the Catholic Lord Stafford, who was imprisoned on Oates's accusations in October 1678 and condemned on Oates's evidence in December 1680. See 1 Sam. xv. 32-33.

PAGE 51. THE MEDALL. Shaftesbury was indicted on a charge of high treason on 24 November 1681 (cf. *Absalom and Achitophel*, introductory note). The biased jury returned the bill marked *Ignoramus*; and the London rabble celebrated the Whig victory with bonfires, 'insolence and riot'. A medal was struck in commemoration: the obverse carries a bust of Shaftesbury; the reverse a view of London Bridge and the Tower, with the sun breaking through a cloud, and the inscriptions 'Lætamur' and '24 Nov. 1681'. Dryden's satire is said to have been suggested by Charles II and rewarded with 'a present of a hundred broad pieces'.

3. *The Polish Medall.* It was a common Tory joke that Shaftesbury aspired to the throne of Poland in 1675, when Sobieski was elected. Cf. l. 15.

17. *Canting*: puritan, Whiggish.

22. *Style*: the engraver's tool.

24. *his ever-changing Will*. See *Absalom and Achitophel*, l. 1, note.

31. *Vermin*. 'Earwig' was a common metaphor for a whisperer or parasite. *th' Usurper*: Cromwell.

33–41. *He cast . . . interlope*. The Tories made the most of the reputed libertinism of Shaftesbury, and of the hypocritical puritans in his following. 'Some of them are *Atheists*, some *Sectaries*, yet *ALL True Protestants*. *Most* of them love all *Whores*, but her of *Babylon* [the Roman Church] . . . 'tis no matter how a man lives; he is a *Saint* by *Infection* . . . his *wickedness* is no more than *frailty*' (Dryden, *The Vindication*, 1683). *Interlope*: trade without a licence.

56. *convenient*: appropriate, expedient.

59. *Fanatique*: puritan, commonwealth.

60. *gears*: draught harness.

62. *white Witches*: these used their craft to counteract the malignity of black witches. Cf. *The Spectator*, no. 131.

65–66. *our Triple hold*: see *Absalom and Achitophel*, ll. 26–28, note. Dryden echoes the phrases he had used of Shaftesbury in the earlier poem.

67. *Ilium*: Troy, the figure of defeat and destruction by fraud.

73–74. *So Sampson . . . breast*. Judges xvi.

77–80. *When his just Sovereign . . . gale*. To conciliate public opinion on the Dutch war Charles issued a Declaration of Indulgence towards dissenters in 1672. The Commons, suspicious of his motives, forced him to withdraw it; and he undertook to support a Test Bill to require subscriptions to the oaths of allegiance and supremacy, Shaftesbury working to moderate the effects of this on dissenters. This work, and the belief that he was opposed to Charles's French alliance, earned him popularity as a champion of protestantism; and by the end of 1673 he had moved into opposition.

94. *Pindarique*: unrestrained, unregulated, as the style of Pindar was supposed to be. Dryden had described him as a 'wild and ungovernable . . . Poet'. For the metaphor, cf. the political paper *Heraclitus Ridens*, 17 May 1681, '*Pindarick*, which is the Poet's Latitudinarian way of Liberty of Conscience in Verse'.

95–98. *Athens . . . went*. Socrates was executed for impiety, and Phocion on a charge of treason. On each occasion the Athenians repented, and punished the accusers of the condemned man.

100. *the Father . . . the Son*: Charles I, Charles II.

131. *Manna, and . . . Quails*. Num. xi.

147–54. *Our Temp'rate Isle . . . succeeds*. A common theme. Cf. Halifax, *Works*, ed. Raleigh, p. 63: 'Our Government is like our Climate, there are Winds which are sometimes loud and unquiet, and yet with all the Trouble they give us, we owe great part of our Health unto them, they clear the Air. . . . There may be fresh Gales of asserting Liberty, without turning into such storms of Hurricane, as that the State should run any hazard of being Cast away by them.'

162. *Religion thou hast none*. To Shaftesbury is attributed the remark that 'men of sense are really but of one religion' but 'men of sense never tell it'. 'I never heard', says *Heraclitus Ridens* (11 October 1681), 'that he was accused for being of any Religion.'

169. *Stumm*: must, used to renew vapid wine.

171. *the formidable Cripple*. Shaftesbury had a suppurating wound, the consequence of an operation for a cyst of the liver in 1668, which troubled him throughout his life.

210. *surly*: masterful, imperious.

216. *Collatine*: Monmouth. Lucius Tarquinius Collatinus and Brutus drove the Tarquins from Rome and were made first consuls; but Collatine, abominated because he was himself a Tarquin, was forced into exile. Dryden had already warned that a similar fate threatened the Stuart Monmouth: 'the Protestant Successor himself, if he be not wholly governed by the prevailing party, will first be declared no Protestant; and next, no Successor. . . . For all the bustle . . . concerning the Duke of *M*. proceeds from a Commonwealth Principle' (*His Majesties Declaration Defended*, 1681).

PAGE 58. MAC FLECKNOE. The occasion of this satire on the poet Thomas Shadwell, circulating in manuscript by 1678, is unknown. For ten years he and Dryden had been engaged in a literary dispute on rhyme, wit, humour, and other issues. In Dryden's view Shadwell had no understanding of true 'wit' or of the merit of Ben Jonson, whom he professed to imitate. 'I know', said Dryden, 'I honour *Ben Johnson* more than my little Critiques, because without Vanity I may own, I understand him better' (Dedication of *The Assignation*, 1673). This controversy is the basis of *Mac Flecknoe*: Shadwell is portrayed mock-heroically as a literary dunce. But it seems likely that the poem itself was occasioned by a personal quarrel: for Dryden had been carrying on a critical debate for ten years without displaying any animosity towards his opponent, and he later claimed that he seldom resorted to lampoon.

3. *Fleckno*: Richard Flecknoe (d. 1678?), dramatist and poetaster. In the Dedication of *The Kind Keeper* (1680) Dryden points out 'how natural the connection of thought is betwixt a bad Poet and *Fleckno*'.

21–24. *Some Beams . . . Day*. A parody of a passage in Cowley's epic *Davideis*, i:

> Here no dear glimpse of the *Suns* lovely face,
> Strikes through the *Solid* darkness of the place;
> No dawning *Morn* does her kind reds display;
> One slight weak beam would here be thought the *Day*.

Lucid intervall: a period of temporary sanity between fits of lunacy.

29. *Heywood and Shirley*: Thomas Heywood (*c*. 1574–1641) and James Shirley (1596–1666), dramatists. Cf. ll. 100–3.

32–34. *sent before . . . greater name*. Parodying Matt. iii. 3–4. Flecknoe and Shadwell are ironically represented as prophets, priests, and kings of Dulness. Cf. ll. 118–19, 214–17.

33. *Norwich Drugget*: a coarse fabric of wool and linen. Shadwell was Norfolk man.

35. *My warbling Lute*. In *Fleckno, an English Priest at Rome* Marvell describes Flecknoe's 'hideous verse' and his attempts 't' allure me with his Lute'. Shadwell claimed 'some little knowledge' of music, 'having been bred, for many years of my Youth, to some performance in it'.

37–50. *that glorious day . . . Floats along*. Parodying Waller's serious occasional poem *Of the Danger His Majesty . . . Escaped . . . at Saint Andrews*.

42. *in Epsom Blankets tost*: the fate of Sir Samuel Hearty, a coxcomb who 'takes himself to be a Wit', in Shadwell's *The Virtuoso* (1676), II.

47–48. *Pissing-Ally*: probably the passage of that name leading off the Strand. Aston Hall has not been identified.

53–54. *Psyche*: Shadwell's opera, elaborately produced at Dorset Garden in February 1675 with a company of French dancers led by 'the most famous Master' St. André.

57–59. *Singleton*: one of the king's musicians (d. 1686), often employed in the theatre. Villerius is a character in Davenant's semi-opera *The Siege of Rhodes* (1656).

61. *the hopefull boy*: the massive 36-year-old Shadwell. Cowley

speaks of David as an 'innocent *Boy*' in *Davideis*, ii, noting that some make him ten and some as old as thirty-six, 'none of which are contrary to the *Hebrew* use of the word *Boy*' (note 28).

64–65. *Augusta . . . to fears inclin'd*: London in the terror of the Popish Plot. Cf. *Annus Mirabilis*, l. 341.

72–73. *Where their vast Courts . . . sleep*. Parodying Cowley, *Davideis*, i: 'Where their vast *Court* the *Mother-Waters* keep, / And undisturb'd by *Moons* in silence sleep.'

74. *a Nursery*: erected by Lady Davenant in 1671; one of a number of schools for the training of young actors.

76–77. *Where unfledg'd Actors . . . Voices try*. Parodying Cowley, *Davideis*, i: 'Beneath the Dens where *unfletcht Tempests* lye, / And infant *Winds* their tender *Voices* try. . . .'

78. *little Maximins*. Maximin is the ranting tyrant of Rome in Dryden's *Tyrannick Love* (1670).

81. *Simkin*: a simpleton. *The Humours of Simpkin* was a farce current just before Dryden's time; and there may have been others with similar names.

83. *Clinches*: puns.

84. *Panton*: apparently another character in farce.

91–93. Allusions to Shadwell's early plays. In the Preface to *Ibrahim* (1677) Settle refers to *The Humorists* (1671), *The Miser* (1672), and *The Hypocrite* (not otherwise known) as 'three as silly Plays as a Man would wish to see'. Raymond and Bruce are gentlemen of wit in *The Humorists* and *The Virtuoso* (1676) respectively.

94. *Empress Fame*. Cf. Virgil, *Aen*. iv. 173 ff.

101. *Martyrs of Pies*. Cf. Dryden's essay *Of Dramatick Poesie* (1668): 'they have bought more Editions of his Works then would serve to lay under all their Pies at the Lord Mayor's *Christmass*.'

102. *Ogleby*: John Ogilby (1600–76), Scottish dancing-master, Master of the Revels in Ireland and founder of the Dublin theatre, printer, translator, and cartographer. He translated Virgil in 1649, the *Iliad* in 1660, and the *Odyssey* in 1665.

105. *H[erringman]*: Dryden's publisher until 1678, and the publisher of all Shadwell's plays 1673–8.

108–11. *our young Ascanius*, &c. Virgil's 'magnae spes altera Romae' (*Aen*. xii. 168). Dryden parodies *Aen*. ii. 682–4.

112–13. *As Hannibal . . . Rome*: Livy, *Hist*. xxi. 1.

120–1. *In his sinister hand . . . potent Ale*. When the sovereign leaves the

Abbey after coronation, the orb is in the left hand and the sceptre in the right. On Shadwell's love of ale, cf. *The Second Part of Absalom and Achitophel*, p. 64.

122. *Love's Kingdom*: a tragi-comedy by Flecknoe.

126. *Poppies*. This ornament has three significances: the poppy is soporific, parching and sterilizing, and aphrodisiac but not fertilizing.

134-8. *The Syre . . . prophetick mood*. Parodying classical representations of Jupiter and Virgil's description of the Sibyl (cf. *Aen.* x. 113-15; vi. 46-51, 77-82).

144. *all . . . Amen*. Cf. Neh. viii. 6.

147-8. *Success . . . Industry*. Cf. Virgil, *Aen.* xii. 435-6.

149. *Let Virtuoso's . . . be Writ*. In the Prologue to *The Virtuoso* (1676) Shadwell declares that 'Wit, like *China*, should long buri'd lie', and hits at 'Drudges of the Stage' like Dryden who are 'bound to scribble twice a year'.

151. *gentle George*: Sir George Etherege. The following lines refer to his plays: Dorimant, Mrs. Loveit, and Fopling are characters in *The Man of Mode*, Cully in *The Comical Revenge*, and Cockwood in *She wou'd if she cou'd*.

163-4. *But let . . . Epsom prose*. Sedley wrote a poor prologue for Shadwell's *Epsom-Wells* (1673), and was said (to Shadwell's indignation) to have helped with the play itself.

168. *Sir Formal*: 'the greatest Master of Tropes and Figures: The most *Ciceronian* Coxcomb' in *The Virtuoso*: 'he never speaks without Flowers of Rhetorick.'

170. *thy Northern Dedications*. Of Shadwell's nine plays produced by 1678, five were dedicated to the Duke or Duchess of Newcastle.

173-4. *Let Father Fleckno . . . raise*. Cf. Virgil, *Aen.* iii. 342-3.

179-80. *Prince Nicander . . . strain*. Nicander pursues Psyche with 'Industrious Love' and high rhetoric.

181. *sold . . . Bargains*, &c. To 'sell bargains' meant to make a fool of, to make prurient exchanges in conversation. Dryden echoes Sir Samuel Hearty in *The Virtuoso*, ii: 'hold thy peace, with a whip-stitch, your nose in my breech.'

182. *Promis'd a Play . . . Farce*. Cf. Shadwell, Dedication of *The Virtuoso*: 'I have endeavour'd, in this Play, at Humour, Wit, and Satyr. . . . I say nothing of impossible, unnatural Farce Fools, which some intend for Comical, who think it the easiest thing in the World to write a Comedy.'

184. *whole Eth'ridg dost transfuse*: there are merely similarities of situation between *Epsom-Wells* and Etherege's *She wou'd if she cou'd.*

185–6. *so transfus'd . . . below.* 'That *Oyl* mixt with any other liquor, still gets uppermost, is perhaps one of the chiefest *Significancies* in the *Ceremony* of *Anointing Kings* and *Priests*' (Cowley, *Davideis*, iv, note 28).

189–92. *This is . . . thy will.* Parodying Shadwell's Jonsonian definition in the Epilogue to *The Humorists*:

> A Humor is the Byas of the Mind,
> By which with violence 'tis one way inclin'd:
> It makes our Actions lean on one side still,
> And in all Changes that way bends the will.

194. *likeness*: to Jonson. *Tympany*: 'A kind of obstructed flatulence that swells the body like a drum' (Johnson).

195–6. *A Tun of Man*: like Falstaff (*1 Henry IV*, II. iv. 440). *Kilderkin*: fourth part of a tun.

202. *The stronger poison kills the weaker.* Shadwell protested against Dryden's giving him 'the *Irish* name of *Mack*, when he knows I never saw *Ireland* till I was three and twenty years old, and was there but four Months'.

204–8. *mild Anagram . . . ways*: varieties of false wit (cf. *The Spectator*, nos. 61–63). Poems in shapes were common in the seventeenth century; but l. 207 is perhaps a reference to George Herbert's 'Easter Wings' and 'The Altar'.

212–13. In *The Virtuoso*, iii, Bruce and Longvil, 'Gentlemen of wit and sense', dispose of the rhetorical amorist Sir Formal through a trap-door in the very midst of a flight of eloquence.

215–17. *Born upwards . . . Art.* Parodying 2 Kings ii. 9–13. But while Elijah's mantle fell from him as he went up to heaven in the whirlwind, Flecknoe's is returned from below.

PAGE 64. THE SECOND PART OF ABSALOM AND ACHITOPHEL. Lines contributed by Dryden to Nahum Tate's sequel to *Absalom*. Og is Shadwell (see *Mac Flecknoe*, introductory note), who had become a party writer for the Whigs. '*Og* may write against the King if he pleases, so long as he *Drinks* for him', said Dryden; 'and his *Writings* will never do the Government so much *harm*, as his *Drinking* does it *good*: for true Subjects, will not be much perverted by his *Libels*; but the Wine *Duties* rise considerably by his *Claret*' ('*The Vindication*, 1683).

5. *Link*: a boy accompanying him with a 'link' (torch) of pitch and tow.

36. *Doeg*: Elkanah Settle (1648–1724), a court poet and dramatist who passed into the pay of Shaftesbury, and is ridiculed earlier by Dryden in *The Second Part*.

50–51. *But of King David's . . . Absalom*. Cf. 2 Sam. xviii. 32.

PAGE 66. ABSALOM AND ACHITOPHEL. Part of the great dialogue between Absalom, 'Th' Ambitious Youth', and Achitophel, 'Hells dire Agent' (ll. 303–476).

8. *Angells Metal*. The double quibble, common in Elizabethan poetry, on (i) 'angel' and the coin 'angel-noble' (cf. *The Merry Wives of Windsor*, I. iii. 50), and (ii) 'metal' and 'mettle' (cf. *Measure for Measure*, I. i. 47–49).

18. *Wonders*: deliverance from the Plague, the Fire, and the Dutch in 1666—Dryden's *Annus Mirabilis. The Year of Wonders*.

23. *Studious of*: concerned for.

24. *Enclin'd to Mercy*, which is 'enthroned in the hearts of Kings' (*The Merchant of Venice*, IV. i. 193–6). Despite his policy of letting the anti-papist madness run its course, Charles again and again expressed his aversion to blood.

27–28. *What could he gain . . . Sway*. Cf. Charles's speech to the Oxford Parliament in 1681: 'I, who will never use arbitrary government myself, and resolved not to suffer it in others . . . . It is as much my interest . . . as yours, to preserve the liberty of the subject; because the Crown can never be safe when that is in danger.'

32. *The Dog-Star*: Sirius, which was thought to cause great heat on the earth (cf. Virgil, *Georgics*, ii. 353).

37. *Natures Holy Bands*: filial feeling.

41. *require*: seek, ask for.

42. *Prevents*: anticipates.

51. *His Brother*: James, Duke of York, whose 'being a Papist', said the Commons in 1679, 'and the hopes of his coming such to the Crown hath given the greatest countenance and encouragement to the present conspiracies and designs'.

61–70. *Yet oh that Fate . . . a Godlike Sin*. Cf. Introduction, p. 10.

88. *Sanhedrin*: the supreme court and legislative council of the Jews.

93–94. *when his Treasure . . . buy*. 'When he runs out of money, he must pay for the war by selling the remnants of his independence to Parliament.'

115–16. *e'r Saul . . . durst Depose*. The republicans acknowledged God alone as their king, but they were dispossessed by Cromwell.

136. *a Legacy of Barren Land*: probably the Border estates of Monmouth's wife, the Countess of Buccleuch.

137–8. *Perhaps . . . Praise*. Charles II, like David, was a lover of music. What remains of his poetry is as undistinguished as Achitophel implies.

147. *Distance*: reach.

151. *The Prostrate Vulgar . . . Spares*. An ancient belief, derived from Pliny, *Nat. Hist.* viii. 19.

156. *Self-defence . . . Law*. So Hobbes, *Leviathan*, I. xiv: 'The Right of Nature . . . is the Liberty each man hath, to use his own power, as he will himselfe, for the preservation of his own Nature; that is to say, of his own Life.'

157. *Considering time*: time for reflection.

159. *Prevail*: avail. *Occasion*: opportunity.

160. *try*: test, prove.

170. *Like womens Leachery . . . Constrain'd*. Proverbial: cf. Shakespeare, *The Two Gentlemen of Verona*, I. ii. 53–54.

174. *They who possess . . . Laws*. Double-edged; but Absalom has not the wit to see the argument applied to himself. Cf. *The Medall*, l. 216, note.

PAGE 72. RELIGIO LAICI. Occasioned by an English translation (1682) of Simon's *Histoire critique du Vieux Testament*, in which the unreliability of the Hebrew texts was illustrated. Whether Simon 'be realy a *Papist*', said John Evelyn, '*Socinian*, or meerely a *Theist*, or something of all three, is not easy to discover; but this is evident—as for the Holy Scriptures, one may make what one will of them for him. He tells the world we can establish no Doctrine or Principles upon them, and then, are not we of the Reform'd Religion in a blessed condition'. Dryden reviews the problems of belief and of scriptural authority, and argues for the Anglican middle course between the acceptance of authority and the exercise of 'private Reason'. The opening passage (ll. 1–41) and the discussion of authority (ll. 316–456) are given here.

1–11. *Dim . . . Supernatural Light*. Cf. Virgil, *Aen.* vi. 270–1, 'quale per incertam lunam sub luce maligna', &c. The whole passage closely resembles Donne's *Biathanatos*, 'The Third Part of the Law of God', I. i. On Dryden's view of reason see Introduction, pp. 13–14.

18. *interfering*: colliding (Lat. *ferire*).

21. *the Stagirite*: Aristotle, a native of Stageira.

39–40. *How can . . . Infinity*. Cf. *The Hind and the Panther*, ll. 43–44.

61. *disinteress'd*: impartial (cf. Fr. *intéresser*).

65. Some editors read 'best authorities, next rules'. But the phrase may be interpreted as it stands: 'the rules of the best authority (the Fathers), being nearest (next) in time from the original texts.'

72. *provoke*: appeal, especially to a higher ecclesiastical tribunal.

107. *took . . . on Content*: accepted without question.

119. *on Record*: by misrepresenting the written record.

132. *The Spirit . . . Degree*. See *Absalom and Achitophel*, ll. 185–7, note (p. 171).

143–6. *While Crouds . . . Food*. So Butler describes (*Hudibras*, III. ii. 7–12) Religion's spawn of 'Petulant Capricious Sects, / The Maggots of Corrupted Texts'.

179–82. *this unpolish'd . . . serve*. Dryden says in his Preface that 'the Expressions of a Poem, design'd purely for Instruction, ought to be Plain and Natural, and yet Majestick. . . . A Man is to be cheated into Passion, but to be reason'd into Truth.'

PAGE 77. THE HIND AND THE PANTHER. Dryden became a papist in 1685–6. On his view of reason and faith see Introduction, pp. 13–14. The passages given here are from Parts i. 62–149, ii. 515–55, and iii. 1141–91.

1–10. *What weight . . . forsake*. A logical extension of the scepticism of 'private reason' expressed in *Religio Laici*.

17–25. *my doubts . . . rebell*. 'Dryden insists that the Protestant churches, which have consented to postpone human reason to faith by acquiescing in the orthodox doctrine of the Trinity, are not entitled to appeal to the authority which they have waived for arguments against the mystery of the real presence in the eucharist' (Scott).

34–38. *Impassible*: incapable of suffering injury. In natural philosophy 'penetration' is the occupation of the same space by two bodies at the same time. Dryden's example of divine penetration is drawn from John xx. 19.

43–44. *Let reason . . . infinity*. cf. *Religio Laici*, ll. 36–41.

89–129. *Now, to remove . . . age*. A triumphant celebration of the Roman Church.

92–93. *What from . . . spouse*. Rev. xxi. 2.

101. *Entire . . . Diamond*. Cf. Spenser's account of Arthur's shield, made 'all of Diamond perfect pure . . . one massie entire mould' (*The Faerie Queene*, I. vii. 33).

109. *the Gyant-brood*: the offspring of Coelus and Terra, who conspired to dethrone Jupiter and were destroyed with the help of Hercules; here, heretics.

112–21. *like Ægyptian . . . sore*. Exod. viii, ix.

126–9. *The Gospel-sound . . . age*. Dryden was at work on his translation of Bouhours's *Life of St. Francis Xavier*, 'Apostle of the *Indies*, and of *Japan*', published in 1688.

130–80. *A Portly Prince . . . what he is*. A 'character', comparable with the portraits in *Absalom and Achitophel*, of Gilbert Burnet (1643–1715), Scottish historian and after 1688 Bishop of Salisbury. Burnet went into voluntary exile in 1685, and from Holland published an account of his continental travels 'to expose both Popery and Tyranny'. James II was greatly displeased; and Burnet, whom the Dutch refused to extradite, was indicted of high treason in April 1687 (in Scotland) and June (in England). *The Hind and the Panther* appeared in May, at the crisis of Burnet's fortune.

131. *a Son of Anach*. Num. xiii. 33.

135. *form'd . . . Proselyte*. In May 1687 Burnet married a Dutch gentlewoman of Scots extraction. The courtship was known at Whitehall: James, 'understanding that I was like to have one of the best matches in the Hague . . . thought to have broke this by accusing me of high treason.'

143. *a fair Behaviour, and a fluent Tongue*. 'When Burnet preached, part of his congregation *hummed* so loudly and so long that he sat down to enjoy it, and rubbed his face with his handkerchief' (Johnson).

163. *A Greek . . . twice*. Virgil, *Aen*. ii. 49, 'timeo Danaos et dona ferentes.'

168–71. *But he . . . Times*. In April 1675 Burnet disclosed to a committee and in Parliament some remarks which the Duke of Lauderdale had made privately to him. His first intention was 'his Patron to controul': 'I said to some, that Duke *Lauderdale* had gone so far in opening some wicked designes to me, that I perceived he could not be satisfied, unless I was undone.'

170. *Sathan*: in Hebrew, an adversary, one who plots against another.

171. *Moloch*: the Canaanite idol to which human sacrifices were made.

176. *Frontless*: shameless. *Scow'rs*: rampages. The Scourers were one of several bands of wild fellows who created uproar in the London streets at night.

177. *an Indian muck*. The erroneous division of 'amuck' was not uncommon. Cf. Marvell, *The Rehearsal Transpros'd* (1672), i. 59, 'like a raging Indian . . . he runs a mucke (as they call it there) stabbing every man he meets'.

PAGE 83. THE THIRD SATYR OF JUVENAL, One of the pieces contributed by Dryden to a collaborative translation of Juvenal and Persius. This passage (ll. 429–503) translates Juvenal's ll. 268–322, on the dangers of night life in Rome.

12. *scouring*. See *The Hind and the Panther*, l. 176, note.

15. *stern Achilles*. 'The Friend of *Achilles*, was *Patroclus* who was slain by *Hector*' (Dryden).

54. *Padders*: foot-pads.

62. *Beneath the Kings*. '*Rome* was Originally Rul'd by Kings; till for the Rape of *Lucretia*, *Tarquin* the proud was expell'd. After which it was Govern'd by two Consuls, Yearly chosen: but they oppressing the People, the Commoners Mutiny'd; and procur'd Tribunes to be Created; who defended their Priviledges . . .' (Dryden).

70. '*Aquinum*, was the Birth-place of *Juvenal*' (Dryden).

PAGE 86. LUCRETIUS. THE BEGINNING OF THE SECOND BOOK. Published with other translations from Latin and Greek in *Sylvae*, the second part of the miscellany begun by Dryden and his publisher Tonson in 1684.

PAGE 88. TO THE MEMORY OF MR. OLDHAM. John Oldham (1653–83) 'set up for a Wit' in 1681 in London, where he met Dryden, and was later taken into the patronage of the Earl of Kingston. His *Remains* appeared in 1684 with memorial poems by Dryden and others.

9. *Thus Nisus fell*. Virgil, *Aen*. v. 328. Oldham was twenty-two years younger than Dryden; but his *Satyrs upon the Jesuits*, written in 1679, brought him earlier into prominence as a satirist.

11–18. *O early ripe . . . betray'd*. So Dryden, in the essay on satire published with his *Juvenal* (1693), speaks of the imperfections of style in Lucan and Persius, who 'Dy'd before the Thirtieth Year of their Age'.

22–25. *Once more . . . around*. See Virgil, *Aen*. vi. 854–86.

PAGE 92. A SONG FOR ST. CECILIA'S DAY. This and the following poem are odes written for performance with orchestra and chorus at the annual concerts which had been given since 1683 to celebrate St. Cecilia's Day (22 November). The music for *A Song* was composed by Giovanni Baptista Draghi, an Italian organist and music master at court.

It has been analysed by E. Brennecke in *Publications of the Modern Language Association of America*, xlix (1934), 1–36.

1–2. *From Harmony . . . Frame began*. A Platonic doctrine, cf. Job xxxviii. 1–7; Milton, *On the Morning of Christ's Nativity*, ll. 117 ff.; Milton, *At a Solemn Musick*.

8. *Then cold . . . and dry*. Cf. Milton, *Paradise Lost*, ii. 898 and iii. 708–15.

16. *What Passion . . . quell*: the classical doctrine, elaborated by Renaissance theorists, of the emotional 'effect' of music. Cf. *Alexander's Feast*, note.

17. *Jubal*: 'the father of all such as handle the harp and organ' (Gen. iv. 21).

53–54. *An Angel . . . Heaven*. Cf. *Alexander's Feast*, ll. 161–70. In medieval legend St. Cecilia is provided with a guardian angel (cf. Chaucer, *Canterbury Tales*, viii. 152 ff.), here metamorphosed into the spirit of harmony attracted to earth. The association of St. Cecilia with organ music seems to be a Renaissance development of the legend.

61–63. *The Trumpet . . . untune the Sky*. Isa. xxvii. 13; 1 Cor. xv. 52.

PAGE 94. ALEXANDER'S FEAST; OR THE POWER OF MUSIQUE. Written in the autumn of 1697, and performed on 22 November with music (now lost) by Jeremiah Clarke. A second setting was composed by Handel in 1736. 'I am glad to heare from all Hands,' Dryden wrote to his publisher Tonson, 'that my Ode is esteemd the best of all my poetry, by all the Town: I thought so my self when I writ it.' Dryden has combined the story of Timotheus moving Alexander's feelings by music—a stock exemplum of the doctrine of 'effect'—with the other story of Alexander incited by Thais to fire Persepolis, to form a complex dramatic *encomium* of music (see J. Kinsley in the *Review of English Studies*, N.S. iv (1953), 263–7).

25. *The Song . . . Jove*. Virgil, *Ecl*. iii. 60.

30. *Olympia*: Olympias, Alexander's mother. She claimed that he was the son not of Philip of Macedon, but of a supernatural serpent. This added weight to the belief in Alexander's divine origin, and he himself demanded worship as a god.

34. *admire*: wonder at (Lat. *admirari*).

41. *shake the Spheres*. Cf. Virgil, *Aen*. x. 115.

52. *honest*: glorious (Lat. *honestus*).   69. *the Master*: Timotheus.

75. *Darius*: King of Persia, destroyed by Alexander.

95. *'Twas . . . to move*: he had only to move a kindred sound. Cf. Fr. 'il n'y avait qu'à'.

127. *horrid*: rough (Lat. *horridus*).

162. *Vocal Frame*: organ.

163. *Enthusiast*: one divinely inspired.

170. *She drew an Angel down*. See *A Song for St. Cecilia's Day*, ll. 53–54, note.

PAGE 100. THE SECULAR MASQUE. Contributed, with a Prologue and Epilogue, to a revival of Fletcher's play, *The Pilgrim*, which was presented for Dryden's benefit at the end of April 1700. Dryden is said to have died on the third night. The title 'Secular' and the opening lines refer to the turn of the century. 'By the introduction of the deities of the chace, of war, and of love, as governing the various changes of the seventeenth century, the poet alludes to the sylvan sports of James the First, the bloody wars of his son, and the licentious gallantry which reigned in the courts of Charles II and James . . . [In l. 79] there seems . . . to be a secret allusion to the exile of the beautiful queen of James II, so much admired by the Tory poets' (Scott).

3. *the Radiant Belt*: the zodiac.

6. *Fans*: wings (Ital. *vanni*; cf. Milton, *Paradise Lost*, ii. 927).

13. *Momus*: the god of ridicule.

46. *Inspire the Vocal Brass*: sound the war trumpet.

52. *lookt*: stared.

57. *the Tyrian Dye*: blood. The Tyrians were said to have invented purple.

PAGE 106. ANNUS MIRABILIS . . . 1666. Written in Wiltshire in 1666, and designed to show that the year's disasters—the plague, the Great Fire, defeats at sea—were temporary interruptions in England's advance to power and prosperity and had drawn king and people together. Dryden ignores the widespread belief that the fire was the issue of a foreign plot, and represents the naval war against the Dutch as a heroic enterprise (see E. N. Hooker in the *Huntington Library Quarterly*, x (1946), 49–67; J. Kinsley in the *Review of English Studies*, N.S. vii (1956), 30–37). The diction and style of the poem are in the main heroic: 'Virgil,' says Dryden, 'has been my Master in this Poem: I have followed him every where.' The final section of the poem (ll. 837–1216) is given here.

11–12. Dryden compares Ovid, *Meta.* i. 357–8.

21. *this prodigious fire*. On the morning of 2 September 1666 fire broke

out in Pudding Lane, off Thames Street and a little north-east of London Bridge. By night it had burned along the river almost to Queen Hythe, and into the city as far as Cannon Street. On the second day it reached west along the Thames, east to Tower Street, and northwards beyond Cornhill and the Exchange. On the third day it swept north and west to the city walls, destroying Cheapside, the Guildhall, and St. Paul's; and subsided on the fourth day. See W. G. Bell, *The Great Fire*, 1923.

34. *in silence fed.* Cf. Virgil, *Geor.* iii. 565 and *Aen.* ii. 758. Dryden's personification of the Fire owes much to Virgil.

41. *So scapes . . . Jail.* Cf. Virgil, *Geor.* iv. 263.

45. Dryden compares Terence, *Heauton.*, ll. 366–7.

53–56. *The Ghosts . . . voice.* London Bridge lay in the path of the fire on the first night; the gate tower and houses at the northern end were destroyed. The heads of traitors were impaled above the Southwark gate tower. The 'Fanatick Spectres' are the insurgents executed in 1661–2.

78–80. *Some run . . . to the fire.* Leather buckets and ladders were kept in the city churches. Water for fire-fighting was got by cutting the wooden pipes.

81. *a Belgian wind*: a strong north-easter which blew throughout the days of the fire.

85–86. *Key*: quay. Dryden compares Virgil, *Aen.* ii. 312.

90. *the fate of Simoeis.* The river Xanthus, calling on his tributary Simois for help, tried to drown Achilles and was attacked by Hephaestus in flame (Homer, *Iliad* xxi. 305 ff.).

102. *The curling . . . Tyde.* Cf. Virgil, *Aen.* ii. 706.

111–16. *the main body . . . breast.* On the second day the western arm of the fire moved along the river towards the Fleet Ditch and the palace, and houses were pulled down in Whitefriars to arrest its progress.

117. *thick harbingers of smoke.* The curtain of smoke over London is described with awe by observers. Evelyn thought it reached to fifty miles in length, giving the city 'burning, a resemblance of Sodome, or the last day' (*Diary*, 3 September).

137–8. *He sees*, &c. Cf. Virgil, *Geor.* iii. 468–9.

141–52. *The powder . . . fellows meet.* The king acted on the suggestion of 'some stout Seamen' to stop the fire by blowing up houses in its path; but it crossed the gap over pieces of debris and on the strong wind.

172. *the spoils . . . lade*: heap stolen wealth. Vulcan was the gods' smith.

186. *require*: seek again (Lat. *requirere*).

189. *the Vestal fire*. Vesta, in whose temple a fire was kept burning continually, was the Roman goddess of the household and hearth.

193–204. *The most . . . such a King*. Citizens gathered in camps outside the walls, mainly in the open spaces of Moorfields. Charles rode out to them, and, telling them that their calamity was 'immediate from the hand of God', pledged himself to take care of them.

209–24. *O God . . . Land*. Cf. David's prayer in the pestilence, 1 Chron. xxi. 12–17.

230. *spotted deaths*: the Plague of 1665.

233. *frequent funerals*: numerous corpses; imitating Virgil's 'plurima . . . corpora' (*Aen.* ii. 364–5).

261–8. *Nor could . . . by fire*. Laud's plan for the restoration of St. Paul's was frustrated by the Civil War, and the larger part of the cathedral was put to profane uses during the interregnum. The 'Poet's Song' is Waller's poem *Upon His Majesty's Repairing of Paul's* (*c.* 1635). Amphion was said to have built the walls of Thebes by playing on his lyre.

284. *give on*: assault.

305–8. *The Father . . . bread*. Two proclamations on 5 September provided for emergency supplies of bread.

321–4. *Not with . . . went*. Ezra i–iii.

326. *two dire Comets*. Cf. Virgil, *Georg.* i. 488.

329–32. *Now frequent . . . succeed*. A trine is the 'aspect' or relative position of two planets which are 120° (a third part of the zodiac) apart. The trine is a benign aspect, because the rays of the two planets fall obliquely and yield to one another. In malignant aspects their rays collide. Dryden adds the favourable astrological circumstance of the planet Jupiter in ascension.

333. *Chymick*: alchemic, transmuting.

337–40. *Already . . . allow*. Plans for the rebuilding of the city, by Christopher Wren, Evelyn, and others, were prepared immediately after the Fire.

341. *August(a)*: the name of London in the fourth century. Cf. *Mac Flecknoe*, ll. 64–65.

PAGE 119. BAUCIS AND PHILEMON. Translating *Meta*. viii. 617–724. Cf. Swift's free version of the story.

46–47. *Kettle . . . little Seether*: 'parvoque . . . aheno' (l. 645). 'Kettle' was currently used for 'cauldron'.

88. *roasted rear*: lightly cooked.

PAGE 125. THE TWELFTH BOOK OF OVID. Translating *Meta.* xii. 210–53 and 393–428 (ll. 292–354 and 524–76 in Dryden's version).

PAGE 129. THE FABLE OF ACIS ... AND GALATEA. Translating *Meta.* xiii. 750–897.

31. *Simagres*: affected glances.

PAGE 136. THE FIRST BOOK OF THE GEORGICS. Translating *Geor.* i. 311–34 (ll. 419–58 in Dryden's version).

PAGE 138. THE THIRD BOOK OF THE ÆNEIS. Translating *Aen.* iii. 613–83 (ll. 804–97 in Dryden's version).

PAGE 141. THE SIXTH BOOK OF THE ÆNEIS. Translating *Aen.* vi. 264–314, Virgil's account of the underworld (ll. 374–432 in Dryden's version).

PAGE 143. CYMON AND IPHIGENIA. Translating Boccaccio, *Decameron*, v. 1, with a personal prologue (ll. 1–41); and completing *Fables*, Dryden's last considerable work. He expands, ornaments, and emphasizes in translation (e.g. ll. 42–45, 58–60, 93–98, 104–6, 172–4, 331–6, 339–48, 458–61, 464–75, 615–24). He takes more trouble than Boccaccio did over the psychology of Cymon (ll. 83–85, 112–16, 117–28, 133–48, 179–82); representing him as a man of violent passion raised suddenly from brutishness, and trying thus to make his conduct less unprincipled and unconvincing than it is in the original (e.g. ll. 234–5, 238–41, 260–3, 300–3). He gives colour and realism to the character of Iphigenia (e.g. ll. 308–11, 318–21, 350–6, 366–8, 422–4). He increases the speed of the climax: Boccaccio's Cymon has three days to consider Lysimachus's proposal, but Dryden's lovers—men of action—decide to join forces on the wedding day itself. Vividness and spirit are added in the final scene (ll. 560–8, 538–9, 579–80, 598–9, 603–4, 607–8).

1–41. *Poeta loquitur*. A reply to Jeremy Collier, a country cleric and author of *A Short View of the Immorality, and Profaneness of the English Stage* (1698).

39. *Ormond*: the Duchess, to whose husband Dryden dedicated his *Fables*.

48. *sincere*: without alloy.

93–94. *Like Dian ... resort*. A reminiscence of Spenser, *The Faerie Queene*, II. iii. 31.

100. *Cymarr*: a loose light garment. Poetical.

117–22. *Through . . . the Year.* Cf. Virgil, *Ecl.* vi. 31 ff.

145. *in gross*: indiscriminately.

179. *Cudden*: dolt.

237. *of the better Hand*: on the right side.

289. *He reap'd . . . only glean'd.* Cf. Virgil, *Aen.* xii. 662–4; Dryden's *Don Sebastian* (1690), I: 'I mow'd across, and made Irregular Harvest, / Defac'd the Pomp of Battel.'

337. *prevents*: is too quick for.

341. *diff'rent*: carrying her in opposite directions.

397. *theirs*: their countrymen of Rhodes.

399–408. *The Country . . . Day.* Dryden's addition. The maintenance of a standing army was a serious issue between William III and the Commons. Cf. *Epilogue to The Wild Gallant Reviv'd*, l. 25; Tom Brown, *Letters from the Dead to the Living* (1700; ed. Hayward, 1927, p. 239), '. . . our holiday heroes and custard-stormers of Cheapside, those merry burlesques of the art military in Finsbury Fields, who, poor creatures, never meant the destruction of any mortal thing but transitory roast-beef and capon.'

424. *So passive . . . Womankind.* A satiric reference to the Anglican doctrine of passive obedience.

427–8. 'It remained either to drop Cymon or to raise him up once more.'

429, 557. *pleas'd*: was decided.

484. *menage*: manage, husband, conserve (Fr. *ménager*).

539. *provoke*: summon (Lat. *provocare*).

552. *suborn*: provide, prepare for.

559. *required*: demanded.

561. *the Posts were crown'd*: the Roman custom of decorating door-posts in celebrations.

613. *buxom*: pliant.

624. *missive*: missile.